Mountain
Trivia
Challenge

Ralph Storer

THE
MOUNTAINEERS

9 8 7 6 5
5 4 3 2 1

Published by The Mountaineers
1001 SW Klickitat Way, Seattle, Washington 98134

Published simultaneously in Canada by Douglas & McIntyre, Ltd., 1615 Venables Street, Vancouver, B.C. V5L 2H1

Published simultaneously in Great Britain by Cordee, 3a DeMontfort Street, Leicester, England, LE1 7HD

Manufactured in the United States of America

Edited by Linda Robinson
Cover design, book design, and typography by The Mountaineers Books

Cover photograph: El Capitan, Yosemite National Park, California

Library of Congress Cataloging in Publication Data

Storer, Ralph, 1947–
      Mountain trivia challenge / Ralph Storer.
           p.   cm.
      ISBN 0-89886-444-5
      1. Mountaineering—Miscellanea. 2. Mountains—Miscellanea.
I. Title.
      GV200.S76   1995
      796.522'02—dc20
                                                    95-9143
                                                    CIP

♻ Printed on recycled paper

Contents

Introduction 7
Beginner's Lucky Seven 10

1. American Mountains 1 12
2. Famous American Climbers 13
3. American Mountain Ranges 1 15
4. What and Where? 1 16
5. Alaska 17
6. State Highpoints 1 19
7. Potpourri 1 20
8. American Trails 22
9. The Northeast 23
10. Like and Unlike 1 25
11. Mount Whitney 27
12. Potpourri 2 28
13. American Mountains 2 30
14. Devil's Work 32
15. Anagrams 1: American Mountains 33
16. National Parks 35
17. Mount Rainier 36
18. Potpourri 3 38
19. American Mountain Ranges 2 39
20. Yosemite 40
21. American Rock 42
22. State Highpoints 2 43
23. The Numbers Game 44
24. Denali 46
25. Potpourri 4 47
26. Mountains of the World 1 49

27. The Himalayas 1 51
28. Films 1 52
29. Gear 54
30. World Trails 55
31. Potpourri 5 57
32. The Matterhorn 58
33. Like and Unlike 2 60
34. Famous Mountaineers of the World 62
35. Hitting the High Spots 1 .64
36. Camping 65
37. The European Alps 66
38. Potpourri 6 68
39. Literary Connections 1 69
40. Glaciers 71
41. Climbing the Wall 72
42. High Country 74
43. Maps and Navigation 76
44. Mountains of the World 2 77
45. Potpourri 7 79
46. Mount Everest 80
47. It's Cold Outside 82
48. Climbing Partnerships 84
49. Anagrams 2: World Mountains 86
50. Mountain Ranges of the World 1 87
51. Potpourri 8 89
52. Mountain Hazards 90
53. Island Mountains 1 92
54. Canada 93
55. Hitting the High Spots 2 .95
56. Canyon Country 96
57. Potpourri 9 98
58. Mountain Passes of the World 100

59. Like and Unlike 3 102
60. The Andes 104
61. Films 2 105
62. Mountain Fauna and Flora 107
63. Potpourri 10 108
64. Mountains of the World 3 110
65. What and Where? 2 111
66. World Alps 112
67. Literary Connections 2 114
68 Volcanoes 115
69. Potpourri 11 117
70. Mountain Weather .118
71. Mountain Ranges of the World 2 120
72. Island Mountains 2 122
73. The Himalayas 2 123
74. Good Seconds 125
75. Potpourri 12 126

Introduction

Trifles make perfection, and perfection is no trifle.

Michelangelo

When storm clouds sweep over the summits and rain lashes the rock, when water washes off the mountainsides and trails turn to mud, when gales chill exposed flesh and flail at flapping flysheets, take time out and curl up in your sleeping bag with this book. When the days grow short and winter hail rattles against the window panes, put your feet up beside the fire and let this book take you in spirit to the mountains. When the summer sun beats down and induces lethargy, when the car journey to the trailhead seems to go on forever, when you're commuting to work and the long, hard day stretches ahead of you and you wish you were in the mountains, let this book exercise your mind. Prepare yourself for the ultimate mountain challenge—the Mountain Trivia Challenge!

This is a quiz book for people who love mountains and all things associated with them. That means you.

How do I know this? Because if you were not interested in mountains you wouldn't be reading this. Whether you climb the fiercest faces in the depths of winter or take a short hike to the mountain foot on a warm afternoon simply to stand and stare, there is something here for you. You will find quizzes where you can show off your knowledge and others where you can display your ignorance. Some are easy and satisfying, some are harder and more informative, some are curious and interesting. Some will stir your imagination, others will infuriate. Some answers you will know, some you won't, some you'll think you know but don't, some you'll think you don't know but do.

And there are yet others you may not wish to know.

Some people say that there are no easy questions and no hard questions—there are simply those to which you know the answer and those to which you don't. You will be pleased to hear that this book adopts a more user-friendly approach, in recognition of the fact that the field of mountains and mountaineering covers a vast area of knowledge. Clues are given in many cases and, ironically, it is often the topics you don't know that are the most interesting and fun to tackle. Guesswork is encouraged—go for it! The main objective is that you find the quizzes pleasurable. I also hope they will provide as much exercise for the mind as mountains do for the body. If you really want to get in the mood, lace up your boots, shoulder your pack, and break out the Power bars. Before tackling a difficult question it might even be worth roping up and putting the first aid kit on standby in case of a slip.

How you wish to use this book is up to you. It's as suitable for solitary quiz-surfing as it is for head-to-head combat with a rival or as a team game. Scoring is also a matter of personal choice. I suggest two points per correct answer, giving a possible total of twenty per quiz; this will enable you to award yourself one point for a nearly correct answer.

You may wonder how long the research for a book of this nature has taken. The answer is at least twenty years, because that's how long I have been hooked on mountains.

More recently, the singular dedication required to compile the seventy-five quizzes that follow has been so intensive that it will be some time before I can again climb a mountain or read a mountaineering book without questions invading my mind. I have become, in Shakespeare's words, "a snapper-up of unconsidered trifles." I need help!

This plea for help is to be taken literally. I am already collecting data for a second quiz book, and any aid you can provide, dear reader, in the form of quiz topics or even individual questions, will be gratefully received and acknowledged. Write to me at the publisher's address. Finally, some of the information presented herein may be open to minor dispute (estimates of the heights of mountains and lengths of trails, for instance, vary from source to source), but I have done my best to ensure that all the answers are correct. Please let me know if this is not the case.

It remains for me to wish you good luck.

Ralph Storer

Question: Who is Ralph Storer?
Answer: Ralph Storer was born in England a little over fifty yards from where Julius Caesar landed in 55 B.C. (Note: to dispel any ambiguity here—55 B.C. was the date Julius landed; Ralph was born slightly later.) He now lives in Scotland, where he lectures in computing, and is well known throughout the UK as a writer of hiking books. He has hiked extensively in the UK and Europe and feels particularly at home in the Scottish Highlands, but in recent years he has fallen in love with the

mountains of the American West and spends an increasing amount of time there. There are few things that give him more pleasure than to disappear into the wilds of the Rockies for a week or two with nothing but a pack and a partner. This is his first American book. He dedicates it to others who seek answers to their questions.

Beginner's Lucky Seven

 **If you can't answer these, give up now!**

1. Arrange the characters "2K" to spell the name of an 8,000-m Himalayan peak.
2. In which country is Mount Kenya situated?
3. For whom is California's John Muir Trail named?
4. Which mountain range was the subject of Edward Whymper's classic mountaineering book, *Scrambles Amongst the Alps in the Years 1860–69*?
5. Who wrote the classic book on alpine climbing in the 1930s entitled *Gervasutti's Climbs*?
6. For which mountain are the White Mountains of California named?
7. How often is the annual *Alpine Journal* published?

Answers

1. K2 • 2. Kenya • 3. John Muir • 4. The Alps • 5. Gervasutti • 6. White Mountain • 7. Once a year

The Questions & The Answers

1

American Mountains 1

☞ **Name the following American mountains.**

1. It is the second highest mountain in the contiguous US after Mount Whitney.

2. This 10,457-ft California mountain, the world's largest plug volcano and the center of a national park, made a series of 300 eruptions between 1914 and 1921 and is the US volcano most likely to erupt again in the future. Despite its height, there is an easy trail to the summit.

3. The second highest and most difficult mountain in the Oregon Cascades, it is topped by a 400-ft pinnacle.

4. A 9,511-ft Washington peak, it is the highest nonvolcanic mountain in the Cascades.

5. A 14,110-ft Colorado mountain, it has both a road and a railway to its summit.

6. It was the first Rocky Mountain peak to be attempted by an expedition from the east, in 1806. The attempt failed, but the peak was named after the expedition leader, first name Zebulon.

7. It was the first "fourteener" to be climbed in North America, by a party led by botanist Edwin James in 1820.

8. This striking mountain near Idyllwild in California's San Jacinto Mountains lies across Strawberry Valley from Suicide Rock and is a major rock-climbing center.

9. It is a 9,594-ft Glacier National Park landmark that was so named by author James Willard Schultz "simply because of its imposing uplift into the blue."

10. From the Snowbowl at 9,300 ft the normal trail up this state highpoint contours under the Hart Prairie chairlift, switchbacks through dense forest to an 11,800-ft saddle where it meets the Weatherford Trail, then goes left along the ridge to the summit.

Answers

1. Mount Elbert, Colorado ✦ 2. Mount Lassen ✦ 3. Mount Jefferson ✦ 4. Bonanza Peak ✦ 5. Pikes Peak ✦ 6. Pikes Peak ✦ 7. Pikes Peak ✦ 8. Tahquitz Peak ✦ 9. Going-To-The-Sun Mountain ✦ 10. Humphrey's Peak, Arizona

2

Famous American Climbers

☞ **Name the following famous American climbers.**

1. A geographer who made the first ascent of the West Buttress of Denali in 1951 and the first ascent of Ama Dablam in 1961, he reached the summit of Mount Everest in 1963.

2. He is a climber, photographer, and writer who made the first ascent of the South Face of Half Dome in 1970, skied the Karakoram High Route in 1980, and whose visit to the newly accessible

mountains of China in the 1980s resulted in perhaps his best-known book, *Mountains of the Middle Kingdom.*

3. A pioneer of American and Canadian climbing who made 12 first ascents in the Canadian Rockies at the turn of the century, he became the first president of the American Alpine Club.

4. A Swiss-born blacksmith, he used his own pegs in Yosemite to make the first true ascent of The Lost Arrow in 1947 and the first ascent of the North Face of Sentinel Rock in 1950. He died at age 94 in 1993.

5. She was the first American woman to reach the summit of Mount Everest, in 1988.

6. A medical professor, he was joint leader of the expedition that made the first ascent of Nanda Devi in 1936 and led the two unsuccessful American K2 expeditions of 1938 and 1953.

7. The founder of the International Mountaineering School at Leysin, Switzerland, he was killed in 1966 during the first ascent of the Eiger Direct, a route that subsequently was named after him.

8. A professor of political science who in the early part of the twentieth century made the first ascents of the South and Middle Tetons, he became one of the first to complete all the Colorado "fourteeners." His Arête on Crestone Needle is one of America's classic rock routes.

9. One of the best-known climbers of the 1920s and 1930s, she was on the first all-female ascent of the Matterhorn and, with her husband, made the first traverse of the Aiguilles du Diable near Chamonix.

10. A rock climber who made his name in Yosemite in the 1960s on first ascents such as North America Wall and Muir Wall on El Capitan, he went on to become famous as a designer of ice axes.

Answers

1. Barry Bishop (1932-1994) ♦ 2. Galen Rowell (1940-) ♦ 3. Charles Fay (1846-1931) ♦ 4. John Salathé (1899-1993) ♦ 5. Stacy Allison (1958-) ♦ 6. Charles Houston (1913-) ♦ 7. John Harlin (1934-1966) ♦ 8. Albert Ellingwood (1888-1934) ♦ 9. Miriam O'Brien (married Robert Underhill) (1899-1976) ♦ 10. Yvon Chouinard (1938-)

American Mountain Ranges 1

1. Name the only major mountain range in the US that is named for the state in which it lies. It forms part of a national park named after its highest mountain.

2. Which range, named for a prominent rock pinnacle, contains the highest peaks in Montana?

3. Name the range that was called "the range of light" by John Muir and whose name in English means "snowy mountains."

4. Which spectacular Idaho range is named for its jagged peaks and serrated ridges?

5. In which state do the Diamond Mountains stand beside the Ruby Mountains?

6. Which range is so named because it was the first Rocky Mountain range encountered by travelers coming from the east?

7. The Great Smoky Mountains are in North Carolina, but where are the Smoky Hills?

8. Which range is named after Montana's state flower and forms a large part of the border between Montana and Idaho?

9. Name the range that contains 16 mountains over 14,000 ft, including the highest mountain in the state, and is known as "the roof of Colorado."

10. In which states are
    (a) the Boston Mountains?
    (b) the New York Mountains?

Answers

10. (a) Arkansas (b) California
♦ 8. The Bitterroot Range ♦ 9. The Sawatch Range ♦
5. Nevada ♦ 6. The Front Range, Colorado ♦ 7. Kansas
♦ 3. The Sierra Nevada, California ♦ 4. The Sawtooths ♦
1. The Alaska Range (Denali National Park) ♦ 2. The Beartooths

What and Where? 1

☞ **What and where in the US are the following?**

1. Gothics
2. Washington Column
3. The Sphinx

4. Angels Landing
5. The Diving Board
6. Old Man of the Mountain
7. The Red Castle
8. Almost-a-dog
9. Pokomoonshine
10. Cow Heaven

Answers

1. A 4,734-ft mountain in the Adirondacks ♦ 2. A rock formation in Yosemite Valley said to look like a giant sculpture of George Washington ♦ 3. A 13,258-ft peak in the Wind River Range, Wyoming ♦ 4. A 5,790-ft rock tower in Zion National Park ♦ 5. A rock projection at the summit of Half Dome that overhangs Yosemite Valley ♦ 6. A 48-ft natural mountain feature on Cannon Mountain, New Hampshire, that resembles the profile of a human face ♦ 7. A 12,825-ft peak in the Uinta Mountains, Utah ♦ 8. An 8,922-ft mountain in Glacier National Park ♦ 9. A rock climbing area in the Adirondacks ♦ 10. A 4,400-ft viewpoint reached by a 5.5-mi trail in the North Cascades

Alaska

1. Of the 20 highest mountains in the US, how many are in Alaska?

  13?   17?   20?

2. Besides Denali (20,320 ft) there are two other great peaks in the Alaska Range, locally named Sultana

(Denali's woman, 17,004 ft) and Begguya (Denali's child, 14,570 ft). What are their English names?

3. If you were hiking in the Aleutian Islands on a summer's day, what would be the odds of getting sunny weather?

    1 in 5?   1 in 10?   1 in 20?

4. Which ice-covered 14,163-ft volcano, named for a nine-teenth-century explorer, emits steam that heats a research station at its summit?

5. In which national park would you be hiking if you went by boat up Muir Inlet to Wolf Point and climbed White Thunder Ridge to view the McBride and Riggs glaciers?

6. Alaska contains the highest mountains in the US, but if all 50 states were listed in order of decreasing *average* elevation, at what position in the list would Alaska be?

    3rd?   9th?   15th?

7. What are the Gates of the Arctic?

8. Name the small range of spectacular granite peaks in the Alaska Range that is one of North America's finest mountain groups, with Yosemite-like wall climbing on spires such as Serenity Spire and Sunrise Spire.

9. If a climber were to fall into the head of the 12-mi long Mendenhall Glacier near Juneau, how many years would it take for the body to reappear at the snout?

    30?   80?   120?

10. What is unusual about Lake George in the Chugach Mountains?

1. 17 • 2. Mount Foraker and Mount Hunter • 3. 1 in 10 • 4. Mount Wrangell • 5. Glacier Bay National Park • 6. 15th (average height 1,900 ft) • 7. The two peaks, Boreal Mountain and Frigid Crags, that stand as sentinels on either side of the North Fork of the Koyukuk River in the Brooks Range • 8. The Cathedral Spires in the Kichatna Mountains • 9. 80 years • 10. It is self-emptying. It forms behind a dam of ice every winter and empties when the pressure of water bursts the dam.

State Highpoints 1

☞ Here is a list of the ten highest state highpoints. Can you match the highpoint in List 1 with its state in List 2?

List 1

1.	Denali	20,320 ft
2.	Mount Whitney	14,494 ft
3.	Mount Elbert	14,433 ft
4.	Mount Rainier	14,410 ft
5.	Gannett Peak	13,804 ft
6.	Mauna Kea	13,796 ft
7.	Kings Peak	13,528 ft
8.	Wheeler Peak	13,161 ft
9.	Boundary Peak	13,140 ft
10.	Granite Peak	12,799 ft

List 2

    a. Alaska

    b. California

    c. Colorado

    d. Hawaii

    e. Montana

    f. Nevada

    g. New Mexico

    h. Utah

    i. Washington

    j. Wyoming

Answers

1. Denali—Alaska (a) ◆ 2. Mount Whitney—California (b) ◆ 3. Mount Elbert—Colorado (c) ◆ 4. Mount Rainier—Washington (i) ◆ 5. Gannett Peak—Wyoming (j) ◆ 6. Mauna Kea—Hawaii (d) ◆ 7. Kings Peak—Utah (h) ◆ 8. Wheeler Peak—New Mexico (g) ◆ 9. Boundary Peak—Nevada (f) ◆ 10. Granite Peak—Montana (e)

7

Potpourri 1

1. Which state has the highest average elevation (6,800 ft)?
   Alaska?   Colorado?   Wyoming?

2. The Oklahoma hill Canaval is claimed to be the highest hill in the world. Why?

3. Where does a bachelor stand beside a sister in Oregon?
4. What is the claim to fame of Kitt's Peak in Arizona?
5. Approximately how many miles of walking trail are there in the US?

    50,000?   100,000?   200,000?

6. Why is Evolution Basin in California's Sierra Nevada so named?
7. Which wilderness area contains the most remote hiking in the Rocky Mountains? It is named for a pioneer conservationist who worked for the United States Forest Service in the 1920s and 1930s.
8. What is a "herd path" in the Adirondacks?
9. The Heavenly tram climbs to 8,200 ft on Heavenly Mountain. Where?
10. How many "fourteeners" are there in Colorado?

Answers

1. Colorado • 2. It is 1,999 ft high; another foot and it is said that it would become a mountain. • 3. Bachelor Butte stands beside South Sister, the most popular of the trio of Oregon mountains known as the Three Sisters. • 4. It has the largest solar telescope in the world. • 5. 100,000 • 6. Its six surrounding peaks are named for exponents of the theory of evolution: Darwin, Fiske, Haeckel, Huxley, Spencer and Wallace. • 7. The Bob Marshall Wilderness • 8. An unmaintained trail • 9. Lake Tahoe • 10. 54

American Trails

☞ **Match the description in List 1 with the trail in List 2.**

List 1

1. A 100-mi circuit around Mount Rainier
2. A 210-mi trail that begins/ends at the summit of Mount Whitney
3. A 9.5-mi trail that descends 4,400 ft from the South Rim to the bottom of the Grand Canyon
4. A trail from Mount Katahdin, Maine, to Springer Mountain, Georgia
5. An 8-mi trail among the hoodoos of Bryce Canyon
6. A 30-mi trail around Mount St. Helens
7. A tri-state trail that was one of the first National Scenic Trails to be established in 1968
8. A 100-mi trail along the length of the Wind River Range, Wyoming
9. A 94-mi trail across the Pasayten Wilderness, Washington
10. A trail to the wettest place on earth

List 2

a. The Appalachian Trail
b. The Boundary Trail
c. The Bright Angel Trail
d. The Fairyland Loop Trail
e. The Highline Trail
f. The John Muir Trail
g. The Leewit Trail

h. The Pacific Crest Trail

i. The Pihea Trail

j. The Wonderland Trail

Answers

1. The Wonderland Trail (j) • 2. The John Muir Trail (f)
• 3. The Bright Angel Trail (c) • 4. The Appalachian Trail (a)
• 5. The Fairyland Loop Trail (d) • 6. The Leewit Trail (g)
7. The Pacific Crest Trail (h) • 8. The Highline Trail (e)
• 9. The Boundary Trail (b) • 10. The Pihea Trail, Kauai,
Hawaii (i)

The Northeast

1. Name the only two peaks in the Catskills of New York State that are over 4,000 ft high.

2. What is or are the Adirondack Forty-Sixers?

3. What do the following Adirondack peaks have in common?

     Blake   Cliff
     Nye   Couchsachraga

4. On the list of 4,000-ft peaks in the White Mountains of New Hampshire drawn up by the Appalachian Mountain Club in the 1950s to aid peakbagging, how many peaks were there?

5. What do the following White Mountain peaks have in common?

     Galehead   Bondcliff

6. How do you join the Catskill 3500 Club?

7. If you take the Helen Taylor Trail from Roaring Brook Campground to Pamola and then cross the Knife Edge to the South Peak and summit, which peak will you have climbed?

8. Name the northeastern mountain range whose peaks were named for Native American chiefs such as Passaconaway, Wonalancet, Kancamagus, and Osceola.

9. Name the New Hampshire mountain whose several summits are denoted by letters, of which "A" and "E" are over 4,000 ft high.

10. Why is there a large pile of small rocks at the summit of Mount Skylight in the Adirondacks?

Answers

1. Slide Mountain (4,180 ft/1,274 m) and Hunter Mountain (4,040 ft/1,231 m) • 2. (a) The 46 Adirondack peaks originally thought to be over 4,000 ft high when peakbagging began here in the 1920s (b) The club whose members have completed ascents of all 46 4,000-ft peaks • 3. Although still on the list of Forty-Sixers, measurements made since the 1920s have shown them to be less than 4,000 ft high. • 4. 46 • 5. Galehead was measured as over 4,000 ft high in 1975 and Bondcliff in 1982, raising the total of White Mountain 4,000-ft peaks to 48. • 6. By climbing all 35 3,500-ft Catskill peaks at least once, plus 4 named peaks again in winter • 7. Baxter Peak on Mount Katahdin • 8. The Sandwich Range of New Hampshire • 9. Wildcat Mountain • 10. According to tradition, if a hiker does not take a stone up the mountain and leave it at the summit, it will rain.

10

Like and Unlike 1

☞ **What do the following four things have in common?**

1. Cassin Ridge   Catacomb Ridge
   Pioneer Ridge   Reality Ridge
   Clue: Alaska

2. Apollo Temple   Juno Temple
   Jupiter Temple   Venus Temple
   Clue: Arizona

3. Donohue Pass   Mather Pass
   Pinchot Pass   Selden Pass
   Clue: California

4. Arrowhead   Finger of Fate
   Old Smoothie   Split Tooth
   Clue: Idaho

5. Mount Eisenhower   Mount Jefferson
   Mount Monroe   Mount Washington
   Clue: New Hampshire

☞ **Which of the following four things is different from the other three and why?**

6. Half Dome   North Dome
   Quarter Domes   South Dome
   Clue: Yosemite

7. Chief Joseph Mountain   Crazy Horse Mountain
   Sacajawea Peak   The Matterhorn
   Clue: Eagle Cap Wilderness, Oregon

8. Mount Cornell   Mount Harvard
   Mount Princeton   Mount Yale
   Clue: Colorado

9. Granite Mountains   Iron Mountains
   Marble Mountains   Silver Mountains
   Clue: California

10. Mount Churchill   Mount Eisenhower
    Mount Roosevelt   Mount Stalin
    Clue: Alaska Highway

Answers

1. They are all ridges on Denali. ◆ 2. They are all mountains in the Grand Canyon. ◆ 3. They are all passes on the John Muir Trail. ◆ 4. They are all rock towers in the Sawtooth Mountains. ◆ 5. They are all mountains named after presidents in the Presidential Range. ◆ 6. South Dome is the only one that is not a mountain in Yosemite National Park. ◆ 7. Crazy Horse Mountain is the only one that is not a mountain in the Eagle Cap Wilderness. ◆ 8. Mount Cornell is the only one that is not a Colorado "fourteener." ◆ 9. The Silver Mountains are the only ones not in California. ◆ 10. Mount Eisenhower is the only one that is not a mountain in Stone Mountain Provincial Park on the Alaska Highway.

11

Mount Whitney

1. Before Alaska became the 50th state of the union, Mount Whitney (14,494 ft) was the highest peak in the US. At which position on the list of highest peaks is it now?

         6th?   17th?   29th?

2. In which national park does Mount Whitney stand?

3. When Clarence King made his first attempt to reach the summit of Mount Whitney with Richard Cotter in 1864, which mountain did he climb by mistake?

4. When Clarence King made his second attempt to reach the summit of Mount Whitney in 1871, which mountain did he climb by mistake?

5. Clarence King eventually reached the summit of Mount Whitney on his third attempt in 1871, only to discover that he had been beaten to the first ascent by three locals—Charley Begole, Johnny Lucas, and Al Johnson. Why did they make the climb?

6. The three locals who made the first ascent gave Mount Whitney an alternative name based on a popular activity in which they indulged. This name persisted locally for some years and almost became the official name until a bill proposing the change was vetoed by the governor of California. What was this alternative name?

7. The current east side trail from Whitney Portal to the summit of Mount Whitney is 11 mi long and climbs 6,134 ft. When was the first east side trail to the summit constructed?

      1904?   1920?   1936?

8. How many switchbacks are there between Trail Camp, an overnight stop on the trail at 12,039 ft, and Trail Crest at 13,777 ft on the summit ridge?

      53?   96?   130?

9. What is the Peewee?

10. The number of people climbing Mount Whitney each year peaked in the years preceding the introduction of overnight camping restrictions in 1972. How many people reached the summit in 1970?

      5,132?   9,899?   13,417?

12

Potpourri 2

1. Where would you be hiking if you encountered signs with the warnings, "Do not continue unless you have water and food. There is no water for 7 mi. Carry 1

gallon water minimum per person," and "A one-day trip beyond Cedar Ridge should not be attempted except by those with previous hiking experience"?

2. The oldest mountaineering magazine in the US is *Summit*. In which year did it first appear?

  1872?   1931?   1955?

3. What was the last Colorado "fourteener" to be climbed?

4. John Vincent Hoeman, the first man to climb all 50 state highpoints, was killed in an avalanche on Dhaulagiri in the Himalayas in 1969. However, Arthur Harmon Marshall was the first man to climb all the state highpoints. Why?

5. In World War II, climbers enlisted in the First Mountain Infantry Battalion. On which northwest US mountain did the battalion train?

6. How did rancher Will Rogers make the first ascent of the Devil's Tower in 1893?

7. What turned back Fritz Weissner, Bill House and Lawrence Coveney on a reconnaissance for the first "real" ascent of the Devil's Tower in 1937?

8. Which state has the highest average elevation (1,500 ft) east of the Mississippi?

   North Carolina?
   Vermont?
   West Virginia?

9. Why is the Weeping Wall in Glacier National Park so named?

10. Which 4,047-ft peak is named for Thomas Crawford, an early White Mountain guide?

Answers

• 10. Mount Tom
9. A curtain of water showers over its lip in early season.
• 7. A vicious gooseberry bush • 8. West Virginia
• 6. He fixed a ladder to the rock and then climbed the ladder.
• 5. Mount Rainier
1936, when there were only 48 states.
• 3. Crestone Needle • 4. He reached his last highpoint in
• 1. The South Kaibab Trail, Grand Canyon • 2. 1955

13

American Mountains 2

☞ **Name the following American mountains.**

1. The summit of this Alaskan "fourteener," the most difficult 14,000-ft mountain in North America, is the highest of three tops on a 3-mi-wide plateau and is rarely reached by more than half a dozen climbers a year. It was named by New York reporter Robert Dunn for his Aunt Anna in 1903.

2. The name of this 14,162-ft mountain is also the name of a lake, the second largest dam in the US, the largest caves in California, and a ruined gold-mining town.

3. Of all the volcanoes in the Cascade Mountains of the American northwest, only Mount Rainier is higher than this almost perfect cone, which Josiah Whitney climbed in 1862, measured as 14,442 ft high, and declared the highest mountain in the US.

4. Most Colorado mountains can be hiked. The most prominent exception is this 13,113-ft peak, which is capped by a sheer 350-ft volcanic plug.

5. An 1,800-ft volcanic plug that rises fortress-like out of the New Mexico desert, it was regarded as America's toughest climbing problem until it was first climbed in 1939.

6. One of the most difficult state highpoints, it is a 12,799-ft mountain whose summit is normally reached by crossing Froze-to-Death Plateau and climbing the east ridge, with its famous snowbridge.

7. At tree line on this mountain you encounter a sign that says, "STOP! The area ahead has the worst weather in America. Many have died there from exposure, even in summer. Turn back now if the weather is bad."

8. Perhaps the most popular high American mountain for rock climbers, this 13,766-ft Wyoming peak is the highest of three known to French trappers as "the three breasts."

9. An 11,049-ft peak that is the highest point in Death Valley National Monument, it was so named because you cannot see beyond it even with the aid of an astronomical instrument.

10. Trails up the east and west forks of the Little Colorado River meet on the grassy summit ridge of this 11,403-ft peak in eastern Arizona, but the last 0.5 mi to the summit is closed to hikers because the peak is sacred to the Apaches.

Answers

1. Mount Hunter ◆ 2. Mount Shasta ◆ 3. Mount Shasta
◆ 4. Lizard Head ◆ 5. Shiprock ◆ 6. Granite Peak,
Montana ◆ 7. Mount Washington, New Hampshire
◆ 8. Grand Teton ◆ 9. Telescope Peak ◆ 10. Mount Baldy

Devil's Work

☞ **Name the following Satanic mountains and other rock formations.**

1. A 5,117-ft rock monolith in Wyoming, it became the first US National Monument in 1906. In 1941 it was the scene of a famous rescue attempt when a parachutist became stranded on top.

2. An 11,865-ft peak in the Pioneer Mountains of Idaho where the devil may have slept

3. A 9,280-ft peak on the rim of Hells Canyon, Idaho, where the devil may have sat

4. A 7,760-ft pinnacle near the latter, presumably named for the part of the devil's anatomy that it resembles. Also the name of a 9,915-ft pinnacle in the Drakensberg of South Africa

5. A rock formation at Crater Lake, Oregon, named for another part of the devil's anatomy

6. One of the most dramatic peaks in the Alaska Coast Range, a 9,077-ft granite spire named for yet another part of the devil's anatomy. Also the name of a strik-

ing peak on the east coast of Greenland

7. Another dramatic 8,586-ft peak in the Alaska Coast Range not far from the previous peak, either geographically or anatomically

8. A California national monument that is a prime example of columnar fissuring in a basaltic outflow, caused by contraction of lava following cooling

9. An area of Arches National Park, Utah, whose fantastic rock formations would appear to be the devil's plants

10. An area of bubbling volcanic pools in Mount Lassen National Park, California, where it would seem the devil does his cooking

Answers

10. Devil's Kitchen
◆ 7. Devil's Paw ◆ 8. Devil's Postpile ◆ 9. Devil's Garden
4. Devil's Tooth ◆ 5. Devil's Backbone ◆ 6. Devil's Thumb
1. Devil's Tower ◆ 2. Devil's Bedstead ◆ 3. Devil's Throne

15

Anagrams 1: American Mountains

☞ Can you find the names of the American mountains hidden in the following anagrams?

1. TIN PALACE
Clue: a Yosemite landmark (two words)

2. DRAGON TENT
Clue: a Wyoming landmark (two words)

3. THE MOSS TUNNEL

Clue: a Cascades volcano (three words)

4. PARAKEET GIN

Clue: a 12,000-ft Montana peak (two words)

5. BURNT OMELET

Clue: a Colorado "fourteener" (two words)

6. BHUTAN MOOR

Clue: a 12,000-ft Idaho peak (two words)

7. A LACE PEG

Clue: an Oregon mountain that has a wilderness area named for it (two words)

8. AT SAMSON HUT

Clue: a conical California peak (two words)

9. NO TOFU REMARK

Clue: an Alaska "fourteener" (two words)

10. ELEGIAC PARK

Clue: a 10,000-ft peak in the Washington Cascades (two words)

Answers

1. El Capitan ◆ 2. Grand Teton ◆ 3. Mount St. Helens ◆ 4. Granite Peak ◆ 5. Mount Elbert ◆ 6. Mount Borah ◆ 7. Eagle Cap ◆ 8. Mount Shasta ◆ 9. Mount Foraker ◆ 10. Glacier Peak

16

National Parks

☞ **The answer to each of the following questions is the name of an American national park.**

1. Name the region of sharp, rugged peaks that adjoins Waterton Lakes National Park in Canada to form an International Peace Park.

2. Of which national park is Mount Lyell (13,114 ft) the highest mountain?

3. Which national park is named for a range of mountains in the Tennessee Appalachians and is the most visited national park in the US?

4. Name two of the three national parks on the Continental Divide.

5. Where would you be hiking if you walked through Wall Street and past Thor's Hammer on the Navajo Loop Trail? The place is well described by the name by which it was originally known to the Paiute Indians: "unka timpe wa wince pock ich" ("red rocks standing like men in a bowl-shaped canyon").

6. Name the Alaska national park that is the largest in the park system and contains several peaks over 16,000 ft high.

7. Name the densely forested national park in the Blue Ridge Mountains that hikers on the Appalachian Trail cross for 94 mi.

8. Which national park contains two active volcanoes and hiking trails from sea level to over 13,000 ft?

9. Name the Utah national park whose main attraction is the spectacular canyon carved by the Virgin River and guarded by the 6,555-ft Watchman. The 17.5-mi-long canyon narrows provide the classic hike in the park.

10. The highest point on the eastern seaboard is 1,530-ft Cadillac Mountain on Mount Desert Island. In which national park does it stand?

Answers

1. Glacier National Park, Montana • 2. Yosemite National Park, California • 3. Great Smoky Mountains National Park • 4. Glacier National Park, Montana; Rocky Mountain National Park, Colorado; Yellowstone National Park, Wyoming • 5. Bryce Canyon National Park, Utah • 6. Wrangell—St. Elias National Park • 7. Shenandoah National Park, Virginia • 8. Hawaii Volcanoes National Park, Hawaii • 9. Zion National Park • 10. Acadia National Park, Maine

17

Mount Rainier

1. Name the most popular route to the summit of Mount Rainier.

2. When did the first definite ascent of Mount Rainier take place?

    1820?   1870?   1920?

3. How did Mount Rainier gain a foot in 1989?

4. How many glaciers does Mount Rainier have?

      6?   16?   26?

5. What natural warm shelters can be found at the summit of Mount Rainier?

6. Name two of the four major ridge routes up Mount Rainier.

7. Is the volcano that forms Mount Rainier

      active?   dormant?   extinct?

8. Who was Peter Rainier, after whom Mount Rainier was named?

9. To the nearest 1,000, how many people reach the summit of Mount Rainier each year?

      1,000?   2,000?   4,000?

10. What percentage of people who set out to climb to the summit fail to get there?

      25%?   50%?   75%?

Answer

1. The Disappointment Cleaver ("D.C.") route ◆ 2. 1870 ◆ 3. Remeasurement by satellite raised its height from 14,410 ft to 14,411 ft. ◆ 4. 26 ◆ 5. Firn caves, warmed by volcanic fumaroles ◆ 6. Curtis Ridge, Liberty Ridge, Ptarmigan Ridge, Sunset Ridge ◆ 7. Dormant ◆ 8. A Rear Admiral in the British navy. The mountain was given his name by Captain George Vancouver during exploration of the Pacific Northwest coast in 1792. ◆ 9. 4,000 ◆ 10. 50%

37

18

Potpourri 3

1. You might expect to find Alpine Lakes in the Alps, but where will you find them in the US?
2. What is the highest point east of the Rockies?
3. Which 11,901-ft peak in the Tetons is named for a Native American tribe?
4. Where in Idaho can you walk from Heaven to Hell in less than 10 mi?
5. Which state contains the world's largest flat-topped mountain—Grand Mesa?
   Colorado?   New Mexico?   Utah?
6. Name the only Colorado "fourteener" besides Pikes Peak that has a road to its summit.
7. Who were the Vulgarians?
8. When seen from afar, the several tops on the summit ridge of 4,393-ft Mount Mansfield, the highest mountain in Vermont, resemble the features of a face. After which feature is the highest summit named?
9. Name the peak in the St. Elias Mountains that was climbed by a senator in 1968 and named for him.
10. Which is the oldest US climbing club (founded in 1876) still in existence?

Answers

1. The North Cascades, Washington ✦ 2. Harney Peak (7,242 ft), South Dakota ✦ 3. Nez Perce Peak ✦ 4. From Heaven's Gate lookout to the bottom of Hells Canyon ✦ 5. Colorado ✦ 6. Mount Evans ✦ 7. A self-styled group of 1950s Shawangunk climbers who objected to the increasing regimentation of climbing there ✦ 8. The Chin ✦ 9. Mount Kennedy (after Robert Kennedy) ✦ 10. The Appalachian Mountain Club

19

American Mountain Ranges 2

1. Which 110-mi-long range on the Continental Divide, named for a river, is the largest range in Wyoming and contains the highest mountains in the state?

2. Name the so-called "last great wilderness," bordered on its southern edge by the Arctic Circle, that is the greatest east-west range in the US.

3. What is the only major east-west range in the contiguous US, whose name is another term for the Ute Indians?

4. The Black Hills are in South Dakota, but where is the Black Range (highest point Reeds Peak [10,011 ft])?

5. Name the small range of granite peaks that is known as Oregon's Little Switzerland, complete with its own Matterhorn.

6. Name the nearest mountain range to Los Angeles,

whose highest peak, Mount San Antonio (10,064 ft), is also known as Old Baldy.

7. Which range forms the eastern boundary of Yellowstone Park and is named for the Crow Indian word for themselves?

8. Name the major range on Oahu, whose high point is 3,150-ft Konahuanui.

9. In which range (one of the highest and most extensive in the US) is Mount Blackburn (16,390 ft) the highest mountain?

10. In which states are
    (a) the Henry Mountains?
    (b) the Shirley Mountains?

Answers

1. The Wind River Range ♦ 2. The Brooks Range, Alaska ♦ 3. The Uintas, Utah ♦ 4. New Mexico ♦ 5. The Wallowas ♦ 6. The San Gabriel Mountains ♦ 7. The Absaroka Range, Montana ♦ 8. The Koolau Range ♦ 9. The Wrangell Mountains, Alaska ♦ 10. (a) Utah (b) Wyoming

Yosemite

1. How did George Anderson make the daring first ascent of Half Dome in 1871?

2. How did Phimister Proctor make the second, even more daring ascent of Half Dome in 1884?

3. Name the 13,114-ft mountain that is the highest in Yosemite National Park.

4. The maximum group size permitted for on-trail backpacking in the Yosemite backcountry is 25. What is the maximum group size permitted for off-trail hiking?

    4?   8?   25?

5. Name the trail that climbs into Little Yosemite Valley beside 594-ft Nevada Fall and 317-ft Vernal Fall, whose spray forms rainbows, wets hikers, and gives the trail its name.

6. How many days did it take Warren Harding and various partners to make the first ascent of the Nose of El Capitan in 1958?

    15?   30?   45?

7. The North America Wall on the southeast face of El Capitan was first climbed by Royal Robbins, Chuck Pratt, Tom Frost, and Yvon Chouinard in 1964. Why is the wall so named?

8. When was the first climbers' guidebook to Yosemite published?

    1935?   1948?   1963?

9. The trail from Yosemite Valley to Glacier Point is almost 5 mi long, so why is it called Four Mile Trail?

10. What was officially allowed at Glacier Point for the first time in 1974, when 170 occurrences were recorded, and then banned again in 1990?

1. He climbed the rock by fixing a line of bolts, standing on each one in turn, and reaching up and drilling a hole for the next one. • 2. Barefoot, he hauled himself up Anderson's line of bolts by standing on each one and lassoing the next (over a period of 18 months) • 3. Mount Lyell • 4. eight • 5. Trail of Mist • 6. 45 days • 7. It contains a section of black diorite that forms a crude map of the North American continent. • 8. 1963 • 9. When originally completed in 1872, the trail was 4 mi long, and when it was rebuilt and lengthened in 1929 the old name stuck. • 10. Hang-gliding

21

American Rock

☞ **Where in the US are the following rock climbs?**

1. Book of Brilliant Things   Equinox
   Illusion Dweller   The Last Unicorn
2. Athlete's Feat   FM
   Jackson's Wall   Where Eagles Dare
3. Limelight   MF
   Shockley's Ceiling   Vandals
4. Centrefold   Davis-Holland
   Godzilla   Japanese Gardens
5. Community Pillar   Mescalito
   Resolution Arête   Velvet Wall
6. Delirium Tremens   Spank the Monkey
   To Bolt Or Not To Be   Watts Tots
7. Blankety Blank   Fred
   Open Book   The Vampire

8.	Optical Promise	Pink Adrenaline
	The Terminator	Uriah's Heap
9.	Darth Vader's Revenge	Lucky Streaks
	Magical Mystery Tour	Solitary Confinement
10.	Dreamer	Sky Rider
	The Witch Doctor Route	When Butterflies Kiss
		Bumblebees

Answers

1. Joshua Tree, California ◆ 2. Boulder Canyon, Colorado
◆ 3. Shawangunks, New York ◆ 4. Index Town Walls,
Washington ◆ 5. Red Rocks, Nevada ◆ 6. Smith Rock,
Oregon ◆ 7. Tahquitz, California ◆ 8. Hueco Tanks, Texas
◆ 9. Tuolumne Meadows, California ◆ 10. Darrington,
Washington

22

State Highpoints 2

☞ **Here is a list of the ten lowest state highpoints. Can you match the highpoint in List 1 with its state in List 2?**

List 1

1.	Taum Sauk Mountain	1,772 ft
2.	Unnamed	1,670 ft
3.	Cambell Hill	1,550 ft
4.	Unnamed	1,257 ft
5.	Charles Mound	1,235 ft
6.	Jerimoth Hill	812 ft
7.	Woodall Mountain	806 ft

	8.	Driskill Mountain	535 ft
	9.	Tower Hill	448 ft
	10.	Britton Hill	345 ft

List 2

a. Delaware

b. Florida

c. Illinois

d. Indiana

e. Iowa

f. Louisiana

g. Mississippi

h. Missouri

i. Ohio

j. Rhode Island

Answers

1. Taum Sauk Mountain—Missouri (h)   ◆   2. Unnamed 1,670
ft—Iowa (e)   ◆   3. Cambell Hill—Ohio (i)   ◆   4. Unnamed 1,257
ft—Indiana (d)   ◆   5. Charles Mound—Illinois (c)   ◆   6. Jerimoth
Hill—Rhode Island (j)   ◆   7. Woodall Mountain—Mississippi (g)
◆   8. Driskill Mountain—Louisiana (f)   ◆   9. Tower Hill—
Delaware (a)   ◆   10. Britton Hill—Florida (b)

23

The Numbers Game

☞ Fill in the missing numbers. Each number is greater than the number in the preceding question.

1. ____ Dome

   Clue: a Yosemite landmark

2. ___ Point Mountain
   Clue: the name of two Idaho mountains—a 9,426-ft peak in the Salmon River Mountains and a 10,124-ft peak in the Boise Mountains

3. The ___ Sisters
   Clue: glacier-covered 10,000-ft volcanoes in Oregon

4. The ___ Peaks
   Clue: prominent landmarks in southern Arizona

5. Plain of the ___ Glaciers
   Clue: a valley near Lake Louise in the Canadian Rockies

6. The ___ Devils
   Clue: mountains on the rim of Hells Canyon

7. Valley of the ___ Peaks
   Clue: a valley near Lake Louise in the Canadian Rockies

8. ___ Lake Basin
   Clue: a beautiful region of lakes and mountains skirted by the John Muir Trail, California

9. The Valley of ___ Falls
   Clue: a picturesque valley on the flanks of Mount Robson in the Canadian Rockies fed by meltwater from hanging glaciers

10. The Valley of the ___ Smokes
    Clue: a volcanic region in Katmai National Park, Alaska

Answers

- 1. Half ◆ 2. Two ◆ 3. Three ◆ 4. Four ◆ 5. Six
- 6. Seven ◆ 7. Ten ◆ 8. Sixty ◆ 9. A Thousand
- 10. Ten Thousand

24

Denali

1. Denali (20,320 ft) is the Athabascan Indian name for the mountain that from 1896 to 1980 was known as Mount McKinley. What does Denali mean in English?

2. Denali has the highest rise above its surrounding elevations of any mountain on the surface of the earth. To the nearest 2,000 ft, what is the height of its summit above its base?

3. What are the chances of the summit of Denali being free of cloud on any given day from June through August?

    15–20%?   35–40%?   55–60%?

4. How was Dr. Frederick Cook's claimed first ascent of Denali in 1906 disproved?

5. Although Cook lied about reaching the summit of Denali in 1906, he did successfully undertake an unusual expedition in the Denali region in 1909, one that remained unrepeated until 1978. What was the expedition?

6. How did the four sourdoughs who climbed the lower North Peak of Denali in 1910 record their achievement so that no one could question it?

7. The first ascent of the higher South Peak of Denali was finally achieved by a four-man team led by 50-year-old archdeacon Hudson Stock. When?

    1913?   1918?   1923?

8. Name the regular route up Denali, a route of no technical difficulty but one that still involves climbing a 1,000-ft headwall of 40–50° snow and ice between 15,000 ft and 16,000 ft.

9. On the first winter ascent of Denali in 1967, what wind-chill temperatures were encountered?

   -50° F?   -100° F?   -150° F?

10. How much did it cost in 1994 to be rescued from Denali?

   Nothing? $250? $500?

Answers

1. The Great One or High One ✦ 2. 18,000 ft ✦ 3. 35–40% ✦ 4. His faked summit photograph was replicated on a lower peak in 1910. ✦ 5. A land circumnavigation of Denali peak in 1910. ✦ 6. They left a flagpole at the summit. ✦ 7. 1913 ✦ 8. The West Buttress route ✦ 9. -150° F ✦ 10. Nothing

25

Potpourri 4

1. Which state has the most "fourteeners"?
   Alaska?
   California?
   Colorado?

2. Why is Vermont called "The Green Mountain State"?

3. Name the great Lakota (Sioux) leader whose likeness is being carved on a mountain in the Black Hills of South Dakota?

4. Name the rock in Sequoia National Park, California, whose vertiginous summit can be climbed by a winding and exposed rock staircase for a stunning panoramic view of the High Sierra.

5. What is or are "The Adirondack Peeks"?

6. If the heights of the highest points in all fifty states were added together, what would be their combined height?

> 201,429 ft?
>
> 307,963 ft?
>
> 445,531 ft?

7. How many fingers has Jack, according to the 7,841-ft peak named for him beside the Pacific Crest Trail in Oregon?

8. What is the cause of most mountaineering accidents in the US?

9. Why are Helen Lake and Wanda Lake on the John Muir Trail in the Sierra Nevada so named?

10. Which federal agency acts as arbiter for disputes over mountain names?

Answers

1. Colorado ◆ 2. *Vert Monts* is French for Green Mountains, the main range in the state. ◆ 3. Crazy Horse ◆ 4. Moro Rock ◆ 5. A semi-annual journal published by the Adirondack Forty-Sixers peakbagging club ◆ 6. 307,963 ft ◆ 7. Three. The peak is Three Fingered Jack. ◆ 8. A fall or slip on rock ◆ 9. They were the names of John Muir's daughters. ◆ 10. The Board of Geographical Names

Mountains of the World 1

☞ **Name the following mountains of the world.**

1. A 12,388-ft (3,776-m) volcano that is perhaps the most-climbed high mountain in the world, with as many as 20,000 tourists, climbers, and Buddhist pilgrims making the ascent every summer weekend.

2. On July 16, 1741, after a difficult month-long crossing from Russia, Vitus Bering sighted this uncharted mountain and named it after a Russian saint. For many years it was believed to be North America's highest peak, and it took 57 days to make the first ascent in 1897.

3. This 21,130-ft (6,444-m) mountain was known until 1982 as the "Last Virgin of the Khumbu" because it was the last named unclimbed peak in the Mount Everest region.

4. Declared by the 1966 World Conference on Scenic Beauty to be "the most beautiful mountain in the world," this twin-peaked 19,510-ft (5,947-m) Andean mountain is famed for its fluted ice buttresses.

5. An African volcano named for its snowcap, its Swahili name means "the mountain that glitters."

6. An 11,870-ft (3,618-m) mountain that is known as the "Matterhorn of the Canadian Rockies," it was first climbed by British mountaineer James Outram's

party in 1901 after an intense rivalry almost matching
that of the first ascent of its Swiss counterpart.

7. An 11,475-ft (3,498-m) ice-hung peak on New Zealand's
   Main Divide, it was named after the Dutch navigator
   who discovered the island in 1642.

8. This is a 9,573-ft (2,918-m) mountain that is the highest
   in its country. Its highest point is called Mytikas (the
   Point) and one of its subsidiary tops is known as the
   Throne of Zeus.

9. An American mountain, it has the highest unbroken
   rise from base to summit of any mountain in the
   world.

10. A 24,741-ft (7,541-m) mountain that at the end of 1994
    was the highest unclimbed mountain in the world, it is
    the 67th-highest individually recognized mountain in
    the world.

Answers

27

The Himalayas 1

1. The name "Himalaya" comes from the Sanskrit words *hima* and *alaya.* What do they mean in English?

2. How many individually recognized 8,000-m (26,247-ft) peaks are there in the Himalayas?

    9?   14?   23?

3. Mount Everest is the highest 8,000-m peak, but what is the lowest?

4. What is the percentage of oxygen in the air at 8,000 m compared to that at sea level?

    32%?   42%?   52%?

5. K2, coincidentally the second highest mountain in the world, was the second in a list of peaks surveyed by the British in the 1850s. What was the last peak in the list called?

    K13?   K33?   K233?

6. What does the K in K2 stand for?

7. At one time K2 was unofficially known as Mount Godwin-Austen, but the proposal to make the name official was never adopted. Why Godwin-Austen?

8. The government of Nepal recognizes four climbing seasons that can be booked for a mountain. One of these is the monsoon season. Name the other three.

9. What is the approximate average height of Tibet?

   10,000 ft (3,000 m)?

   13,000 ft (4,000 m)?

   16,000 ft (5,000 m)?

10. What is bed tea in the Himalayas?

Answers

trek cooks
delivered to Himalayan trekkers in their tents at dawn by the
post-monsoon, winter. ◆ 9. 16,000 ft (5,000 m) ◆ 10. Tea
surveyor who explored its glaciers in 1861. ◆ 8. Pre-monsoon,
by Colonel Henry Haversham Godwin-Austen, a British military
Everest) ◆ 5. K33 ◆ 6. Karakoram. ◆ 7. K2 was first sighted
(26,360 ft/8,035 m) ◆ 4. 32% (26% at the summit of Mount
1. Snow (hima) abode (alaya) ◆ 2. 14 ◆ 3. Gasherbrum II

28

Films 1

1. In which film does Clint Eastwood go rock climbing in Utah in preparation for a climb in the Swiss Alps?

2. In *First Blood,* how does Rambo escape from pursuing cops when trapped on a cliff face?

3. In which film does Scotland's Ben Nevis stand in for the surface of Jupiter?

4. Which 1935 film climaxes with the eruption of a volcano, courtesy of the special effects team responsible for *King Kong*?

5. In *Deadly Pursuit,* how do Sidney Poitier and Tom Berenger survive a blizzard in the Cascades?

6. On which Australian rock outcrop did a group of schoolgirls disappear during a Valentine's Day picnic in 1900?

7. Through which region of buttes, mesas, and canyons did John Wayne pursue Natalie Wood in 1956?

8. How does Sean Connery's alpine guide meet his end in *Five Days One Summer*?

9. Which mountain plays the part of the Citadel, climbed by Michael Rennie and James MacArthur in *Third Man on the Mountain* in 1959?

10. Relaxing between space missions, Captain Kirk goes solo rock climbing on earth in *Star Trek V.* On which peak is he climbing when he falls and has to be rescued by Mr. Spock in anti-gravity boots?

Answers

• 1. *The Eiger Sanction* • 2. He jumps, aiming for a tree to break his fall. • 3. 2001. The transformation was achieved with the aid of aerial photography and psychedelic coloring. • 4. *The Last Days of Pompeii* • 5. They dig a snow hole. • 6. Hanging Rock. The film is *Picnic at Hanging Rock.* • 7. Monument Valley, Utah. The film is *The Searchers.* • 8. He is killed by rockfall. • 9. The Matterhorn, Switzerland • 10. El Capitan in Yosemite National Park, California

Gear

1. Why are Vibram soles so called?

2. Which is better for off-trail hiking and why: a pack with an internal frame or a pack with an external frame?

3. What is or was a star mugger?

4. On the first ascent of Mount Logan, Canada's highest peak, in 1928, how much did the sleeping bag of each member of the party weigh?

    2 lbs?   10 lbs?   17 lbs?

5. Where did the rubber come from in the original "sticky" rock-climbing boots made by the Spanish manufacturer Boreal?

6. What is a Gamow bag?

7. Carabiners were first used by Austrian climbers in the 1900s. From where did they get the idea?

8. In traditional boot construction, Norwegian stitching is normally used to attach uppers to soles. What is Norwegian stitching?

9. What was unusual about the clothes worn by Sherpa Lopsang Janbu on his ascent of Mount Everest in 1994?

10. International safety standards for climbing equipment are laid down by the UIAA What do the initials UIAA stand for?

Answers

1. They were invented by Vitale Bramani in Italy in 1935. ◆ 2. A pack with an internal frame, which allows a more contoured fit and a lower center of gravity to improve balance on off-trail terrain ◆ 3. A type of nail used on the soles of boots before rubber soles were invented ◆ 4. 17 lbs ◆ 5. Recycled aircraft tires ◆ 6. A portable pressure chamber made from Kevlar for use at high altitude ◆ 7. The Munich fire brigade ◆ 8. Uppers are turned out to form a lip, which is attached to the sole by a double row of stitches. ◆ 9. He dressed in Bakhu, the traditional Sherpa wear, instead of high-altitude clothing. ◆ 10. Union Internationale des Associations d'Alpinisme

30

World Trails

☞ Name the following important long-distance trails of the world.

1. The most famous trail in South America, it is a 3–5 day hike from the train stop known as Kilometer 88 out of Cuzco, Peru, to the Inca ruins of Machu Picchu.

2. It is the best known trail in New Zealand, a 34-mi (54-km), 4-day route in Fiordland National Park that links the Clinton and Arthur Valleys.

3. A challenging 47-mi (75-km), 5–8-day coastal trail on Vancouver Island, Canada, it was originally built to enable shipwrecked sailors to reach safety.

4. It is an 11-day loop trail that circumnavigates the highest mountain in the Alps.

5. A 33-mi (53-km), 3–5-day trail, dubbed "the longest museum in the world," it retraces the route of the Klondike Gold Rush stampeders across Alaska's coastal mountains.

6. A 53-mi (86-km), 6–7-day loop trail, it circles a group of spectacular Patagonian mountains in the southernmost national park in Chile.

7. Australia's best known trail, it is a 56-mi (91-km), 5–8-day hike through Tasmania's Cradle Mountain–Lake St. Clair National Park.

8. It is one of a network of trans-European long-distance trails that crosses Europe for about 1,240 mi (2,000 km) from Ostend in Belgium to Nice on the French Riviera.

9. It is a 32-mi (51-km), 3-day trail that circumnavigates a 22,028-ft (6,714-m) Tibetan holy mountain where pilgrims usually outnumber trekkers.

10. A 260-mi (420-km) trail in British Columbia, Canada, it is named for the first white man to reach the Pacific Ocean from the east in 1793.

Answers

1. The Inca Trail ♦ 2. The Milford Track ♦ 3. The West Coast Trail ♦ 4. The Tour du Mont Blanc ♦ 5. The Chilkoot Trail ♦ 6. The Torres del Paine Circuit ♦ 7. The Overland Trail ♦ 8. The E2 ♦ 9. The Mount Kailas Circuit ♦ 10. The Alexander Mackenzie Trail

31

Potpourri 5

1. How much of the earth's 56-million-sq.-mi (145-million-sq.-km) land mass is above 3,000 ft (900 m)?

    5%?   15%?   25%?

2. Who was the first man to reach a height of 5,000 m (16,400 ft) on a mountain?

3. What is a Tyrolean traverse?

4. What is the height of the South Pole?

    0 ft (0 m)?   211 ft (63 m)?   9,186 ft (2,801 m)?

5. Why should you not use biodegradable soap in a river?

6. In which languages did the following words originate?

    (a) Anorak

    (b) Cagoule

7. How did King Albert I of Belgium meet his end in the mountains in 1934?

8. In 1953, the year that Mount Everest was first climbed, the highest known seamount (submarine mountain) was discovered between Samoa and New Zealand. How high does it rise above the ocean bed?

    15,500 ft (4,650 m)?

    28,500 ft (8,700 m)?

    36,500 ft (11,100 m)?

9. For what would a double sheet bend be used?
10. What is the world governing body of mountaineering called?

Answers

32

The Matterhorn

1. If the alpine 4,000-m (13,124-ft) peaks are listed in order of decreasing height, ignoring multiple and secondary summits, at what position in the list is the Matterhorn (4,476 m/14,688 ft)?

      5?   10?   20?

2. The Matterhorn was first climbed in 1865. By whose party?

      Chris Bonington's?
      Albert Mummery's?
      Edward Whymper's?

3. How did the first party let a rival Italian party on the mountain know they had reached the summit first?

4. Approximately how many people have climbed the Matterhorn?

    10,000?   50,000?   100,000?

5. What is the greatest age difference between the oldest and youngest person to have reached the summit of the Matterhorn on the same day?

    45 years?   55 years?   65 years?

6. What award did Austrian climbers Franz Xavier Schmid and Toni Schmid receive for the first ascent of the north face of the Matterhorn in 1931?

7 When Jean-Marc Boivin made the fastest-ever solo ascent of the north face of the Matterhorn in 4 hr, 10 min in 1980, how did he descend from the summit?

8 What is the fastest recorded ascent of the Matterhorn (via the Hörnli Ridge)?

    1 hr, 3 min?   2 hr, 7 min?   3 hr, 1 min?

9 What is noteworthy in alpine history about the Hörnli Hut, situated at 10,700 ft (3,260 m) at the foot of the Hörnli Ridge?

10 The Matterhorn straddles the Swiss-Italian border and is known in English by its Swiss name, but what is its Italian name?

Answers

1. Ten ◆ 2. Edward Whymper's ◆ 3. They bombarded them with rocks. ◆ 4. 100,000 ◆ 5. 65 years, between a 76-year-old man and an 11-year-old girl ◆ 6. A gold medal at the 1932 Olympic Games ◆ 7. By hang-glider ◆ 8. 1 hr, 3 min ◆ 9. It was the first alpine hut. ◆ 10. Il Cervino

Like and Unlike 2

☞ **What do the following four things have in common?**

1. Flat Top   Ghent
   Laila   Sickle Moon
2. Mauna Kea   Mount Palomar
   Mount Stromlo   Mount Wilson
3. 29,029 ft (8,848 m)   28,253 ft (8,612 m)
   28,208 ft (8,595 m)   27,890 ft (8,501 m)
4. 1953   1954
   1955   1956
   Clue: first ascents
5. Chiodo   Haken
   Pin   Piton

☞ **Which of the following four things is different from the other three and why?**

6. Broad Peak   Cho Oyu
   Manaslu   Trisul
   Clue: heights
7. Jebel (Morocco)   La (Nepal)
   Shan (China)   Sgurr (Scotland)
8. Cordillera Blanca   Cordillera Falsa

Cordillera Negra   Cordillera Roja

Clue: Andes

9. Abseil   Flash

   Redpoint   Second

10. Aconcagua   Ararat

   Kilimanjaro Popocatepetl

   Clue: volcanic activity

Answers

1. They are all mountains in the Karakoram. • 2. They all have observatories on them. • 3. The mountains with these heights (Everest, K2, Kangchenjunga, and Lhotse) are the four highest mountains in the world. • 4. They are the years in which the four highest mountains in the world were first climbed, surprisingly in order of decreasing height. • 5. They are all the same piece of climbing equipment—a metal blade that can be hammered into a rock crack for protection (*chiodo*—Italian, *haken*—German, *pin*—American, *piton*—French, and *peg*—English) • 6. They are all 8,000-m (26,247-ft) mountains except Trisul (7,120 m/23,294 ft). • 7. They are all names for a mountain except La, which is a name for a mountain pass. • 8. The Cordillera Blanca is a mountain range in the Peruvian Andes. The others don't exist. • 9. They are all methods of climbing rock except abseil, which is a method of descending. • 10. They are all volcanoes, but Popocatepetl is the only one that is not extinct.

34

Famous Mountaineers of the World

☞ **Name the following famous mountaineers of the world.**

1. He is the Italian mountaineer who was the first person to climb all the 8,000-m (26,247-ft) peaks.

2. An American climber who founded the International Mountaineering School at Leysin, Switzerland, he was killed in 1966 during the first ascent of the Eiger Direct, a route that was subsequently named after him.

3. A French climber, famous for her solo rock-climbing exploits, in 1994 she became the first woman to solo the three classic north faces of the Alps in winter (Eiger 1992, Grandes Jorasses 1993, Matterhorn 1994).

4. An Austrian, he is the only person still living to have made first ascents of two 8,000-m peaks (Broad Peak and Dhaulagiri).

5. The Austrian who was the only other person to have made first ascents of two 8,000-m peaks (Broad Peak and Nanga Parbat), he was killed on the descent from Chogolisa in 1957 when he fell through a cornice.

6. A Polish climber who was the first woman to climb K2, she reached the summit of seven other 8,000-m peaks, and disappeared on Kangchenjunga in 1992.

7. The British mountaineer who was perhaps the foremost alpinist of his generation, he wrote the classic *My Climbs in the Alps and Caucasus*, and disappeared while attempting Nanga Parbat in 1895.

8. An Italian climber, he made the first ascent of Gasherbrum IV and numerous peaks in the Andes, but he is best known for his alpine achievements, which include first solo ascents of the Southwest Pillar of the Dru (now named after him) in 1955 and the Matterhorn North Face Direct in 1965.

9. The Polish mountaineer who was the second person to climb all the 8,000-m peaks, he was killed in a fall while climbing Lhotse in 1989.

10. The Japanese mountaineer who climbed Mount Everest in 1970, he was famous for his solo ascents and solo Arctic journeys. He disappeared in 1984 while descending from a winter solo ascent of Denali, Alaska.

Answers

• 1. Reinhold Messner (1944–) • 2. John Harlin (1934–66) • 3. Catherine Destivelle (1960–) • 4. Kurt Diemberger (1932–) • 5. Hermann Buhl (1924–57) • 6. Wanda Rutkiewicz (1943–92) • 7. Alfred Mummery (1855–95) • 8. Walter Bonatti (1930–) • 9. Jerzy Kukuczka (1948–89) • 10. Naomi Uemura (1942–84)

35

Hitting the High Spots 1

☞ Match each mountain in List 1 with the country in List 2 of which it is the highest mountain.

List 1

1. Bourgplatz (1,834 ft/559 m)
2. Carrantuohil (3,414 ft/1,041 m)
3. Chirripo (12,533 ft/3,820 m)
4. Gerlach (8,711 ft/2,655 m)
5. Grossglockner (12,457 ft/3,797 m)
6. Katherina (8,651 ft/2,637 m)
7. Königstein (8,480 ft/2,585 m)
8. Rysy (8,199 ft/2,499 m)
9. Tajumulco (13,845 ft/4,220 m)
10. Zugspitze (9,718 ft/2,962 m)

List 2

a. Austria
b. Costa Rica
c. Egypt
d. Germany
e. Guatemala
f. Ireland
g. Luxembourg
h. Namibia
i. Poland
j. Slovakia

Answers

9. Tajumulco—Guatemala (e) ◆ 10. Zugspitze—Germany (d)
7. Königstein—Namibia (h) ◆ 8. Rysy—Poland (i) ◆
5. Grossglockner—Austria (a) ◆ 6. Katherina—Egypt (c)
1. Bourgplatz—Luxembourg (g) ◆ 2. Carrantuohil—Ireland
(f) ◆ 3. Chirripo—Costa Rica (b) ◆ 4. Gerlach—Slovakia (j)

36

Camping

1. What is a geodesic tent?
2. How does a flysheet increase the warmth of a tent?
3. Most tent frames are attached to the inner tent, as this allows maximum internal volume and allows the inner to be used without a flysheet. Some tent frames, however, are attached to the flysheet and the inner is hung from them. What advantage does this have?
4. On a cold night, which is the warmer place to camp and why: in a depression or on a nearby hillside?
5. What type of tent is a dunnel?
6. If using a groundsheet that is not attached to the tent, should it have a smaller surface area than the bottom of the tent or should it be larger and extend under the tent sides? Why?
7. Does a sleeping bag increase the warmth of its occupant and, if so, how?

8. Which is warmer on a winter's night and why: a light-colored or dark-colored tent?

9. When camping in winter, should snowmelt for drinking be collected at night or in the morning? Why?

10. In the 1970s in the US Jack Stephenson produced tents that could be used without sleeping bags. What was the principle behind them?

Answers

1. A dome-shaped tent whose poles intersect to form triangular and hexagonal panels, producing a strong tent with a high internal volume ◆ 2. It traps insulating dead air. ◆ 3. The inner can be pitched and dismantled dry in wet weather. ◆ 4. On a nearby hillside, because cold night air flows downhill into the depression. ◆ 5. A cross between a dome and a tunnel, combining the internal space of a dome with the aerodynamic qualities of a tunnel. ◆ 6. Smaller, so that condensation from tent walls does not drip onto it. ◆ 7. No, a sleeping bag can only *maintain* warmth for a certain amount of time. ◆ 8. A light-colored tent. Dark colors radiate heat more readily at night. ◆ 9. At night, because snowmelt freezes overnight ◆ 10. They used multiple layers of fabric that created insulating dead-air spaces between them.

37

The European Alps

1. What is an alp?

2. Excluding multiple and secondary summits, how many peaks in the Alps are over 4,000 m (13,124 ft) high?

15?   52?   81?

3. What and when was the Golden Age of Alpinism?
4. Approximately how many climbers' huts are there in the Alps?

    100?   500?   2,000?

5. What is the Haute Route?
6. How was a successful ascent of Mont Blanc celebrated in Chamonix in the nineteenth century?
7. How many routes (including variants) are there on the north face of the Eiger?

    3?   9?   21?

8. The Walker Spur, first climbed in 1938 after numerous failed attempts, is one of the most famous climbs in the Alps. On which mountain is it?
9. What is unusual about the last pitch of the Aiguille de République in the Mont Blanc range?
10. What is the origin of the name of the Viereselsgrat ("Four Asses Ridge"), a ridge of the Dent Blanche first climbed in 1882 by a party guided by Ulrich Almer?

Answers

1. A grassy pasture below the snowline where animals are taken to feed in summer ◆ 2. 52 ◆ 3. The period between the first ascent of the Wetterhorn in 1854 and the first ascent of the Matterhorn in 1865, when nearly all the highest peaks were climbed for the first time ◆ 4. 2,000 ◆ 5. A climbers' route from Chamonix to Zermatt over high mountain passes ◆ 6. By firing cannons ◆ 7. Nine ◆ 8. The Grandes Jorasses ◆ 9. It is climbed by lassoing the top of the Aiguille (pinnacle). ◆ 10. Almer thought he and his three companions were asses for attempting it.

Potpourri 6

1. Which national park has the highest average elevation of any national park in the world?

2. What is it forbidden to wear in an alpine climbers' hut?

3. The highest sea stack in the world is 1,840-ft (560-m) Ball's Pyramid. Where is it?

4. The third ascent of Ball's Pyramid was made by a French team in 1985. Why was it the last?

5. Teiichi Igarashi is the oldest person to have climbed Mount Fuji (12,388 ft/3,776 m) in Japan. To the nearest ten years, how old was he when he reached the summit in 1986?

6. What is a hanging valley and what causes it?

7. What makes the little-known summit of Thabant-shonyana (the Little Black Mountain) in Lesotho a mountain of note, a fact not discovered until 1951?

8. The ancient Greek philosopher Empedocles made one of the first recorded ascents when he committed suicide on a mountain top. How?

9. What is Cheyne-Stokes respiration?

10. Where, outside France, is Mont Blanc (11,800 ft/3,600 m) the highest mountain in the Alps?

altitude • 10. On the moon
high by caused breathing Irregular .9 • Italy, Etna, Mount
of crater the into jumped He .8 • Kilimanjaro. of south
Africa in mountain highest the is it (m 3,482) ft 11,425 At .7
glacier former s'valley main the of power erosive greater
the to owing valley main the of above lies floor whose
valley tributary truncated A .6 • days 302 years, 99 .5 •
UNESCO. through agreement international by prohibited
now is rock the on Landing .4 • Australia of coast
the off (km 700) mi 435 Sea, Tasman the In .3 • boots
Climbing .2 • Nepal, Park, National (Everest) Sagarmatha .1

39

Literary Connections 1

1. Which mountain appears in the title of and provides the backdrop to a 1938 Ernest Hemingway short story that was made into a 1952 film starring Gregory Peck?

2. Name the fictional illusory peak that gives Thomas Mann's 1924 Nobel-Prize-winning novel its symbolic title.

3. Name the world's oldest mountaineering journal, which was first published by the (British) Alpine Club in 1863 and is still published annually.

4. In *The Dharma Bums*, Jack Kerouac describes a beatnik ascent of a mountain in Yosemite National Park, California. Which mountain?

5. Which flat-topped, cliff-encircled 9,219-ft (2,810-m) Venezuelan mountain inspired Sir Arthur Conan Doyle to write *The Lost World*?

6. Who was the subject of James Ramsay Ullman's 1965 biography, called *Man of Everest* in the UK and *Tiger of the Snows* in the US?

7. Name the fictional 40,000-ft (12,200-m) Himalayan mountain that is climbed accidentally by the expedition porters in W. E. Bowman's classic 1956 parody of expedition books.

8. According to Felice Benuzzi's 1952 book, the ascent of which mountain was no picnic for him and his fellow Italians when they escaped from a World War II prisoner-of-war camp in North Africa in order to do some climbing?

9. Name the prophet/teacher in Friedrich Nietzsche's influential 1883 philosophical work who returns to civilization to spread his wisdom after ten years of solitary living in a mountain cave.

10. Who wrote *The Seventh Grade* (1974), *The Challenge, Two Men Alone at 8,000 Metres* (1977), and *Solo—Nanga Parbat 1978* (1980)?

Answers

1. Killimanjaro. The story was called *The Snows of Killimanjaro*. • 2. *Der Zauberberg (The Magic Mountain)* • 3. The Alpine Journal Norgay • 4. The Matterhorn • 5. Roraima • 6. Sherpa Tenzing Norgay • 7. Rum Doodle. The book was *The Ascent of Rum Doodle*. • 8. Mount Kenya. The book was *No Picnic on Mount Kenya*. • 9. Zarathustra. The book was *Also Sprach Zarathustra (Thus Spake Zarathustra)*. • 10. Reinhold Messner

Glaciers

1. What percentage of the earth's land surface is currently covered by glaciers?

    4%?   11%?   20%?

2. Glaciers can be classified as one of three types according to their location. Piedmont and Valley are two of these types. What is the third and most common?

3. What causes a fissure known as a crevasse in the surface of a glacier?

4. Why is it less dangerous to walk on a glacier if it is *dry*?

5. What is a bergschrund?

6. The longest single glacier in the northern hemisphere is the Hubbard Glacier in Alaska, which is 75 mi (120 km) long, but in the Karakoram two glaciers combine to achieve a length of 76 mi (122 km). Name one of them.

7. What is an ice bollard and what is it used for?

8. What is unique about the glacier that formed in the collapsed caldera of Mount Katmai, Alaska, following the eruption of 1912?

9. What is a nunatak?

10. Name the process of glacial ablation in which slabs of glacier ice are broken off at a coastline to float away as icebergs.

Answers

1. 11% ♦ 2. Ice cap or icefield ♦ 3. When a glacier flows over a rise or down a drop, its surface stretches and cracks open. ♦ 4. A dry glacier is one whose surface is not covered by snow and whose crevasses are easily seen. ♦ 5. A large crevasse at the head of a glacier that separates flowing ice from the stagnant ice or rock above ♦ 6. The Hispar and the Biafo ♦ 7. A "mushroom" of ice cut into an ice surface with the aid of an ice axe for use as an abseil anchor ♦ 8. It is the only glacier whose date of origin is known. ♦ 9. An isolated mountain peak that projects through the surface of an ice cap ♦ 10. Calving

Climbing the Wall

☞ **All the questions in this quiz are about great mountain walls of the world.**

1. One of the largest mountain faces in the world is a 4-mi (6-km) wide wall that rises 14,000 ft (4,300 m) from the Peters Glacier to the 19,470-ft (5,934-m) North Peak of Denali, Alaska. It is named after the Alaskan judge who in 1903 made the first attempt to climb Denali, but the wall itself was not climbed until 1963. Name it.

2. One of the classic walls of the Alps is the 4,600-ft (1,400-m) north face of a 13,025-ft (3,970-m) Swiss peak. It has been called the *Mortwand* (Death Wall) because of the many climbers who have died on it. Name the mountain.

3. Which 26,247-ft (8,000-m) peak is named for its 10,000-ft (3,050-m) pale limestone walls? Its name means "Shining Wall" in English.

4. One of the most controversial big-wall routes ever climbed was Warren Harding's and Dean Caldwell's 27-day siege of El Capitan in Yosemite Valley, California, in 1970, during which they refused a rescue attempt by helicopter. Name the route.

5. The largest vertical cliff face in Europe is a 4,000-ft (1,200-m) rock wall that is the most popular rock-climbing area in Norway. Name it.

6. The western side of Kilimanjaro's summit sports a 4,000-ft (1,200-m) wall of steep rock that was first climbed direct by Reinhold Messner in 1978. Name the wall.

7. The longest wall climb in the world is the 14,800-ft (4,500-m) Rupal Flank—of which mountain?

8. The most conspicuous feature in the huge Bob Marshall Wilderness in Montana is a 123-mi (198-km) long, 1,000-ft (300-m) limestone wall on the Continental Divide of the US. Name it.

9. The Canadian Continental Divide west of Banff is formed by a 25-mi (40-km) long, 3,000-ft (900-m) limestone wall along whose foot a popular trail runs from Floe Lake. Name the wall.

10. John Middendorf and Xavier Bongard took 18 days in 1992 to achieve perhaps the most difficult big-wall rock climb ever done. On which Karakoram mountain?

Answers

1. The Wickersham Wall • 2. The Eiger • 3. Gasherbrum IV
• 4. Wall of the Early Morning Light (Dawn Wall) • 5. The Troll
Wall • 6. The Breach Wall • 7. Nanga Parbat • 8. The
Chinese Wall • 9. The Rockwall • 10. Great Trango Tower

High Country

☞ **The answer to each of the following questions is the name of a country.**

1. Name the only landlocked country through which the Andes pass.

2. Ice-capped mountains occur near the equator in three places. The Andes and East Africa are two of these places. Where is the third?

3. Which European principality has no land lower than 3,000 ft (914 m)?

4. Which country contains the most individually recognized 8,000-m (26,247-ft) peaks?

   India?   Nepal?   Pakistan?

5. In which country is Gunong Kerbau (7,159 ft/2,182 m) the highest peak in the Main Range, which itself is the highest of several ranges that run southwards from the Thai border?

6. Where does the British Empire mountain range stand beside the United States mountain range?

7. First ascents of the Himalayan 8,000-m peaks were made by mountaineers from Austria, China, France, Germany, Italy, Japan, Switzerland, the UK, and the US. Which country produced the most first ascents?

8. Which country consists mainly of the limestone mass of Monte Titano (2,382 ft/725 m) and is the world's smallest republic?

9. Three-quarters of this country consists of a 500-mi (800-km) wide east-west heartland bordered on the south by the Siwalik Range, but mountaineers flock here to climb the mountains to the north. Which country?

10. Which country mounts more overseas mountaineering expeditions than any other?

Answers

1. Bolivia ◆ 2. New Guinea ◆ 3. Andorra ◆ 4. Nepal (8 out of 14) ◆ 5. Malaysia ◆ 6. Canada (Ellesmere Island) ◆ 7. Austria (3); France, Switzerland, the UK (2 each); others (1) ◆ 8. San Marino ◆ 9. Nepal ◆ 10. Japan

Maps and Navigation

1. Where were contour lines invented?

2. When contour lines appear close together on a map they indicate a steep slope. What other information is required in order to estimate *how* steep?

3. On a 60° slope, how much is the actual ground distance when the map distance is 200 m?

   200 m?   300 m?   400 m?

4. How can you determine your location by the process of resection (taking back-bearings)?

5. If you follow a bearing of 210° and decide to reverse your route, what will be your new bearing?

6. At midday local time on a sunny day, how can you determine direction without a compass?

7. How can you determine direction on a sunny day without a compass if you don't know the time?

8. How can you determine direction using (a) moss, or (b) an alder?

9. Name the only star in the northern hemisphere that does not apparently change its position in the sky, whatever the time of night and whatever the day of the year, and is thus useful for night navigation.

10. How can the constellation of Orion help you determine direction at night in the northern hemisphere?

1. On Schiehallion (3,553 ft/1,083 m) in the Scottish Highlands. The idea came to Charles Hutton during a survey of the mountain by the British Astronomer Royal in 1774. ◆ 2. The size of the contour interval. ◆ 3. 1,312 ft (400 m) ◆ 4. Take bearings on two or more identifiable features and draw lines from them on the map back along the bearings; where the lines intersect is your location. ◆ 5. 30° ◆ 6. The shadow cast by an object indicates north and south. In the northern hemisphere the tip of the shadow indicates north; in the southern hemisphere it indicates south. ◆ 7. Place a stick in the ground and mark the tip of its shadow at intervals throughout the day. A line connecting these points runs in an east-west direction. ◆ 8. (a) There is more moss on the north side of rocks in the northern hemisphere, and vice versa in the southern hemisphere. (b) An alder's bark is lighter on the south side in the northern hemisphere, and vice versa in the southern hemisphere. ◆ 9. Polaris (the Pole Star or North Star) ◆ 10. It rises in the east and sets in the west.

44

Mountains of the World 2

👉 **Name the following mountains of the world.**

1. An 18,481-ft (5,663-m) mountain on the Georgia/Russia border, it is sometimes called the highest mountain in Europe.

2. A 15,318-ft (4,669-m) mountain on the US/Canadian border that is the highest summit in the Glacier Bay area, it was named, perhaps in jest, by Captain Cook in 1778.

3. A 22,208-ft (6,769-m) Peruvian mountain, it became infamous in 1970 when an earthquake-triggered landslide on its slopes killed all 15 members of a Czech climbing expedition and buried the town of Yungay together with most of its 20,000 inhabitants.

4. A 25,645-ft (7,817-m) mountain, it was the first 25,000-ft summit ever reached, by Noel Odell and Harold (Bill) Tilman in 1936. Willi Unsoeld named his daughter for the mountain and, tragically, she died near its summit on her father's 1976 expedition.

5. Access to this 13,642-ft (4,158-m) mountain, the third highest in the Bernese Alps, is eased by a railway that climbs through the Eiger to a col at 11,722 ft (3,573 m).

6. The only major Canadian Rocky Mountain that is named for one of Canada's ten provinces, it is 11,874 ft (3,619 m) high and was first climbed in 1925 by a team from Japan.

7. A 9,958-ft (3,035-m) peak, known as the "Matterhorn of the South," it is the highest mountain in New Zealand's Haast Range.

8. A well-named, flat-topped 3,566-ft (1,087-m) landmark that is the home of South African rock climbing, it was first climbed in 1503 by the Portuguese admiral Antonio da Saldanha in order to determine his whereabouts.

9. A 23,406-ft (7,134-m) mountain in the Pamirs, it is perhaps the easiest and certainly the most climbed 7,000'er in the world.

10. A 27,605-ft (8,414-m) summit that at the end of 1994 was the highest unclimbed summit (as opposed to sep-

arate mountain) in the world, it is the tenth-highest individually recognized summit in the world.

Answers

* 10. Lhotse Middle Peak
7. Mount Aspiring • 8. Table Mountain • 9. Pik Lenin
* 4. Nanda Devi • 5. The Jungfrau • 6. Mount Alberta
* 1. Mount Elbrus • 2. Mount Fairweather • 3. Huascaran

45

Potpourri 7

1. Why was Mount Cook, the highest mountain in New Zealand, 12,349 ft (3,764 m) high at the end of 1990 but only 12,315 ft (3,753 m) high at the end of 1991?

2. What would you be doing if indulging in *langlauf*?

3. The highest and longest cable car in the world rises to the summit of a 15,629-ft (4,763-m) mountain. Where?

4. How did Voltaire explain the presence of seashells on mountain tops?

5. What is the real reason for the presence of seashells on mountain tops?

6. What did George Leigh Mallory fill his pockets with on Mount Everest?

7. Where and when did modern avalanche control begin?

8. What do rock climbers do when they use combined tactics?

9. Which is Europe's deadliest mountain, with 32 deaths on it between 1989 and 1994?

    The Eiger (Switzerland)?

    Ben Nevis (Scotland)?

    Mont Blanc (France/Italy)?

10. Where on a mountain would you see a *tsunami*?

Answers

1. An avalanche in December 1991 reduced its height by 34 ft (10.4 m). ◆ 2. *Langlauf* is the European term for cross-country skiing. ◆ 3. From Mérida City to the summit of Pico Espejo, Bolivia, a rise of 10,250 ft (3,124 m) ◆ 4. He thought they were carried there by pilgrims. ◆ 5. Sedimentary rocks are formed from the shells and skeletons of sea animals, which are deposited on the sea bed and uplifted. ◆ 6. Sugar lumps ◆ 7. In the Dolomites in World War I, when alpine troops used shellfire to trigger avalanches on the enemy ◆ 8. One stands on the other to reach a hold. ◆ 9. Ben Nevis ◆ 10. Hopefully nowhere; it is the correct name for what is commonly called a tidal wave.

46

Mount Everest

1. Who was Sir George Everest, for whom Mount Everest was named in 1865?

2. The height of Mount Everest is usually given as 29,029 ft (8,848 m). When it was first measured by a British survey team in 1852, however, it was given a height of 29,002 ft. How was this figure obtained?

3. To the nearest thousand, how many hikers per year trek to Everest Base Camp at 17,500 ft (5,350 m) in Nepal?

    5,000?   10,000?   20,000?

4. Who made the first solo ascent of Mount Everest in 1980, a feat made even more astounding by the fact that he used no additional oxygen?

5. In 1988 Marc Batard made the fastest ever ascent of Mount Everest by the southeast ridge. How long did it take him to get from base camp to summit?

    15 hr?   22 hr?   30 hr?

6. How did Jean-Marc Boivin descend from Mount Everest in 1988?

7. Until 1993 American Dick Bass was the oldest person to climb Mount Everest, reaching the summit in 1985 when he was 55. How old was Ramon Blanco, a Spanish guitar maker living in Venezuela, when he became the oldest person to reach the summit on October 7, 1993?

    56?   60?   63?

8. Although Sherpa Ang Rita only began climbing at the age of 30, he has reached the summit of Mount Everest more times than anyone else, always without additional oxygen. When he reached the summit on May 16, 1993, at the age of 45, how many ascents of Everest had he made in total?

    8?   10?   12?

9. On May 10, 1993, a record number of climbers reached the summit of Mount Everest in a single day. How many?

      20?   30?   40?

10. How many known ascents did Mount Everest receive in the forty years between its first ascent on May 29, 1953, and May 29, 1993?

      153?   575?   842?

Answers

1. A former Surveyor General of India (who pronounced his name *Eve-rest*) ◆ 2. The mountain was measured six times and each measurement produced a different height. The average came to exactly 29,000 ft, which it was thought no one would believe, so 2 ft were arbitrarily added to produce the final figure. ◆ 3. 5,000 ◆ 4. Reinhold Messner ◆ 5. 22 hr ◆ 6. By hang-glider. ◆ 7. 60 ◆ 8. Eight ◆ 9. 40 ◆ 10. 575

It's Cold Outside

1. Why are toes and fingers the first parts of the body to succumb to frostbite in cold weather?
2. Which is warmer and why: gloves or mittens?
3. Why is it important to wear a hat in cold weather?
4. What is (a) the best and (b) the next best insulation from the cold?

5. Why are loose clothes warmer than tight clothes?

6. What insulating material has the most warmth, has the least weight, and is the most compressible?

7. The best underwear in cold weather situations is that which absorbs least moisture from the body by wicking it to the next layer of clothing. Match the fiber on the left with its absorbency rate from the list on the right (lowest is best).

Fiber	Absorbency rate
Chlorofiber/Polypropylene	0.3%
Cotton	0.5%
Silk	5.0%
Polyester	8.0%
Wool	17.0%

8. Why should you not drink alcohol when you are cold?

9. If, while hiking, you were to fall into a lake whose water was at freezing point, how long would you survive?

   0–1/2 minute?
   1/2–3 minutes?
   3–5 minutes?

10. Why is it colder in winter than summer?

Answers

1. The process of vasoconstriction constricts blood vessels in the extremities. This reduces blood flow to the fingers and toes and allows them to cool, thereby reducing the amount of body heat lost from them to the air. ♦ 2. Mittens. By separating the fingers, gloves increase the area and therefore the amount of heat loss. ♦ 3. Vasoconstriction does not work in the head and up to 75% of bodily heat can be lost there. ♦ 4. (a) A vacuum; (b) a still gas, e.g., air ♦ 5. Because they can trap warm air next to the skin ♦ 6. Down ♦ 7. Chlorofiber/Polypropylene (0.3%), Cotton (8.0%), Silk (5.0%), Polyester (0.5%), Wool (17.0%) ♦ 8. Because alcohol dilates (opens) blood vessels, thereby increasing blood flow and heat loss by a process opposite to that of vasoconstriction. ♦ 9. ½–3 minutes ♦ 10. The earth is closer to the sun in winter than in summer, but it has a 23.5° tilt. In a northern winter the northern hemisphere is tilted away from the sun and receives less direct solar rays; the reverse is true in the southern hemisphere.

Climbing Partnerships

☞ Name the following famous pairs of climbers.

1. The two men who may have been the first to reach the summit of Mount Everest in 1924, they disappeared on the northeast ridge and never returned to tell the tale.

2. They were the first pair to definitely climb Mount Everest in 1953, via the southeast ridge.

3. An American doctor and a philosophy professor, they became in 1963 the first to traverse Mount Everest.

4. An Austrian and an Italian, they were the first to climb Mount Everest without oxygen, via the southeast ridge in 1978.

5. Two Frenchmen who were the first to climb an 8,000-m (26,247-ft) peak when they reached the summit of Annapurna in 1950, they both were badly frostbitten during an epic retreat from the mountain.

6. An American aunt and nephew, they made countless notable ascents together in the Alps until the former's death in 1876.

7. Two British mountaineers and explorers who pioneered small lightweight expeditions in the Himalayas in the 1930s, they also made the first traverse of Mount Kenya in 1930.

8. A hunter and a doctor from Chamonix, they made the first ascent of Mont Blanc in 1786.

9. They were two pioneer Yosemite climbers of the 1950s who, following an unsuccessful attempt on the unclimbed northwest face of Half Dome in 1955, became members of rival teams in 1957. One eventually succeeded in climbing the face and the other hiked to the summit to greet him.

10. They were two British mountaineers who, after joint exploits that included the first ascent of the West Wall of Changabang and the first ascent without oxygen of the north ridge of Kangchenjunga, disappeared while attempting the unclimbed northeast ridge of Mount Everest in 1982. An award for mountain literature, named after them, commemorates their writing skills.

Anagrams 2: World Mountains

☞ **Can you find the names of the famous mountains of the world hidden in the following anagrams? Words such as "The" and "Mount" may or may not be included.**

1. BURT MONSOON
   Clue: Canada (two words)

2. ALAMO PAY
   Clue: Peru (one word)

3. I GET HERE
   Clue: Switzerland (two words)

4. RUM IS POIGNANT
   Clue: New Zealand (two words)

5. MEANT YUKON
   Clue: Kenya (two words)

6. NET AMOUNT
   Clue: Italy (two words)

7. TOP PEOPLE ACT
   Clue: Mexico (one word)

8. NAILED
   Clue: USA (one word)
9. O IS KNOCKOUT SUM
   Clue: Australia (two words)
10. DIRE PUTT
    Clue France (two words)

Answers

1. Mount Robson • 2. Alpamayo • 3. The Eiger •
4. Mount Aspiring • 5. Mount Kenya • 6. Mount Etna
• 7. Popocatepetl • 8. Denali • 9. Mount Kosciusko
• 10. Petit Dru

50

Mountain Ranges of the World 1

☞ **Name the following mountain ranges of the world.**

1. The second of Western Europe's great mountain ranges after the Alps, it stretches from sea to ocean and contains more than 50 peaks over 10,000 ft (3,000 m) high.

2. A 250-mi (400-km) long mountain range whose name is Turkish for "Black Rubble," it lies parallel to the main crest of the Himalayas at its western end and contains some of the world's highest mountains, including 8,000-m (26,247-ft) peaks such as Broad Peak and Gasherbrum.

3. A heavily glaciated mountain range on the Pacific coast of British Columbia, it contains the highest mountain in Canada, Mount Logan (19,520 ft/5,951 m).

4. The most northerly mountain range in Africa, with a heavy winter snow cover at the edge of the Sahara Desert, its highest peak is Toubkal (13,665 ft/4,165 m).

5. A bleak mountain range around the headwaters of the River Oxus, it contains Pik Communism (24,551 ft/7,483 m), the highest mountain in the former USSR. The range's name actually refers to the valleys that separate individual mountain groups.

6. Literally the "Home of the Giants," this mountain range contains Norway's highest peaks.

7. A range of glaciated peaks in the northwest US, it is best known for its ten major volcanoes.

8. A Turkish mountain range that forms a high barrier between the central Anatolian plain and the Mediterranean Sea, its highest peak is Kaldi Dag (12,251 ft/3,734 m).

9. The highest and most extensive mountain range in Australia, it borders the Pacific Ocean for 600 mi (1,000 km).

10. The most extensive mountain range in Greece, its highest peak is Mount Smolikas (8,639 ft/2,633 m).

Answers

1. Pyrenees • 2. Karakoram • 3. Coast Range • 4. Atlas • 5. Pamirs • 6. Jotunheimen • 7. Cascades • 8. Taurus • 9. Great Dividing Range • 10. Pindus

51

Potpourri 8

1. What is unusual about the rivers of the Tien Shan mountains in central Asia?

2. Why did many early alpinists object to the use of crampons?

3. Running and cycling are two of the three events in the New Zealand Coast to Coast multi-endurance race across the mountains of the South Island. What is the third event?

4. As a shelter from the elements, what is the only dome that can be built without a scaffold?

5. What does Triple Divide Mountain in Glacier National Park, Montana, divide?

6. How long does the trek from the base to the summit of Kilimanjaro and back normally take?

   3 days?   5 days?   7 days?

7. A mountain biker successfully sued Yosemite National Park, California, for $3.6 million when she fell and became paralyzed after riding past a "closed to bikers" sign. What were the grounds for the award?

8. The Houston Everest Expedition of 1933 made history when they flew their Westland aircraft over the summit of Mount Everest. In what did Leo Dickinson fly over Everest on his historic 1991 flight?

9. How thick is Goretex™?

0.1 in (0.254 cm)?

0.01 in (0.0254 cm)?

0.001 in (0.00254 cm)?

10. The Sea of Rains is bordered by the Jura, Alps, Caucasus, Appenine, and Carpathian mountain ranges. Where is it?

Answers

1. None of them reach the sea ♦ 2. They thought that using them was cheating. ♦ 3. Canoeing ♦ 4. An igloo ♦ 5. Streams that flow to three different destinations: the Atlantic Ocean, the Pacific Ocean, and Hudson's Bay ♦ 6. 5 days ♦ 7. It was adjudged that the sign had failed to warn that the trail was dangerous. ♦ 8. A balloon ♦ 9. Only 0.001 in (0.00254 cm), which is why it must be bonded to other material ♦ 10. On the moon

52

Mountain Hazards

1. For which mountaineering affliction was gunpowder solution an old remedy?

2. Why does sunburn occur more rapidly at high altitude?

3. Which of the following actions is the best preventive measure to take against being struck by lightning on a mountain?

(a) Shelter in a small cave or beneath a boulder.

(b) Lie down flat in the open.

(c) Sit on a rucksack in the open.

4. Why are people buried by avalanches usually found near the surface rather than deeper down?

5. Name three ways of decontaminating polluted water for drinking.

6. What should you do if you encounter *appui* while hiking?

7. If you happen to be skiing on the Whakpapa ski-field on Mount Ruapehu in New Zealand and an alarm goes off, why should you get out of there fast?

8. A blizzard is characterized by winds greater than 60 km/hr (37 mph) and temperatures lower than -6°C (21°F). How long does it take exposed flesh to freeze in a blizzard?

   1 minute?   2 minutes?   5 minutes?

9. What is the International Distress Signal, first proposed by the Alpine Club in 1894, and now universally adopted?

10. When Hannibal hiked across the Alps to invade Rome in 218 B.C., what natural hazard destroyed his army?

Answers

53

Island Mountains 1

☞ The following mountains are the highest mountains on the ten largest islands in the world. Can you name the islands?

1. Gunnbjorn's Feld (12,140 ft/3,700 m)
   Size of island: 840,000 sq. mi (2,176,000 sq. km)

2. Puncak Jaya (16,025 ft/4,884 m)
   Size of island: 316,856 sq. mi (820,657 sq. km)

3. Mount Kinabalu (13,455 ft/4,094 m)
   Size of island: 286,967 sq. mi (743,254 sq. km)

4. Massif du Tsaratanana (9,437 ft/2,876 m)
   Size of island: 227,000 sq. mi (587,930 sq. km)

5. Tête Blanche (7,074 ft/2,156 m)
   Size of island: 183,810 sq. mi (476,068 sq. km)
6. Kerinci (12,485 ft/3,805 m)
   Size of island: 182,866 sq. mi (473,623 sq. km)
7. Fujiyama (12,388 ft, 3,776 m)
   Size of island: 88,930 sq. mi (230,329 sq. km)
8. Ben Nevis (4,406 ft/1,344 m)
   Size of island: 88,756 sq. mi (229,878 sq. km)
9. Golden Hinde (7,220 ft/2,200 m)
   Size of island: 82,119 sq. mi (212,688 sq. km)
10. Unnamed (US Range) (8,540 ft/2,603 m)
    Size of island: 81,390 sq. mi (212,119 sq. km)

Answers

1. Greenland ✦ 2. New Guinea ✦ 3. Borneo ✦ 4. Madagascar ✦ 5. Baffin (Canada) ✦ 6. Sumatra ✦ 7. Honshu (Japan) ✦ 8. Great Britain ✦ 9. Victoria (Canada) ✦ 10. Ellesmere (Canada).

54

Canada

1. What was the first North American mountain range to attract alpine mountaineers from Europe in the nineteenth century?
2. Mount Logan (19,520 ft/5,951 m), Canada's highest mountain, was first climbed in 1925. What event inspired the Alpine Club of Canada to attempt it?

3. Mount Logan was not climbed for a second time until 1950. What was noteworthy about Norman Read's successful ascent during this expedition?

4. Which prominent 11,792-ft (3,954-m) mountain in the Canadian Rockies is called *Yuh-hai-has-kun* by the native people because of its appearance? The name means "mountain of the spiral road" and refers to the mountain's sedimemtary layers.

5. Which mountain is named for the one-legged 22-year-old cancer victim who attempted to run a "Marathon of Hope" across Canada in 1981?

6. The largest icefield in the Canadian Rockies covers 125 sq. mi (325 sq. km) and is more than 1,000 ft (300 m) thick. On or around it are found 11 of the 22 highest peaks in the Canadian Rockies. Name the icefield.

7. There are five national parks in the Canadian Rockies. Name three of them.

8. Which hike was voted Canada's best hike in 1981, and still is promoted as such?

9. Wishbone Arête and Emperor Ridge are renowned for their ice gargoyles. They were not climbed until 1955 and 1961, respectively. On which mountain are they?

10. Which famous mountain scene is depicted on the back of a Canadian $20 note?

♦ 10. The Valley of the Ten Peaks
Waterton Lakes National Park ♦ 9. Mount Robson
Kootenay, Waterton Lakes ♦ 8. The Crypt Lake hike in
♦ 6. The Columbia Icefield ♦ 7. Banff, Jasper, Yoho,
expedition. ♦ 5. Mount Terry Fox
1950, he had also reached the top during the successful 1925
Everest in 1924 ♦ 3. Aged 60 when he made the summit in
1. The Selkirks ♦ 2. Mallory's and Irvine's attempt on Mount

55

Hitting the High Spots 2

☞ Match each mountain in List 1 with the country in List 2 of which it is the highest mountain.

List 1

1. Botrange (2,277 ft/694 m)
2. Celaque (9,348 ft/2,849 m)
3. Cerro Aripo (3,088 ft/941 m)
4. Kebnekaise (6,965 ft/2,123 m)
5. Kekes (3,330 ft/1,015 m)
6. Mount Apo (9,700 ft/2,956 m)
7. Tahat (9,575 ft/2,918 m)
8. Vaalserberg (1,053 ft/321 m)
9. Victoria Peak (3,681 ft/1,122 m)
10. Yding Skovhoj (568 ft/173 m)

List 2

    a. Algeria

    b. Belgium

    c. Belize

    d. Denmark

    e. Honduras

    f. Hungary

    g. Netherlands

    h. Philippines

    i. Sweden

    j. Trinidad

Answers

1. Botrange—Belgium (b) ◆ 2. Celaque—Honduras (e)
◆ 3. Cerro Aripo—Trinidad (j) ◆ 4. Kebnekaise—Sweden (i)
◆ 5. Kekes—Hungary (f) ◆ 6. Mount Apo—Philippines (h)
◆ 7. Tahat—Algeria (a) ◆ 8. Vaalserberg—Netherlands (g)
◆ 9. Victoria Peak—Belize (c) ◆ 10. Yding Skovhøj—Denmark (d)

56

Canyon Country

☞ All the questions in this quiz are about great canyon hikes of the world. The answer to each question is the name of a canyon, gorge, or deep valley.

1. The deepest canyon in the US, its river flows 8,913 ft (2,716 m) below He Devil mountain. It has over 900 mi (1,450 km) of maintained hiking trails.

2. The best-known canyon in Mexico, its deepest point is almost 7,550 ft (2,300 m) below the surrounding plateau. The trek to the Rio Urique in the canyon bottom is becoming increasingly popular with adventurous hikers.

3. On the 10-mi (16-km) descent of this celebrated Cretan gorge, hikers pass through the Iron Gates, where the walls of the gorge narrow to 10 ft (3 m), to reach the Mediterranean Sea. The gorge is named for an abandoned village hidden in its depths.

4. Another Greek gorge that has claims to being the deepest narrow gorge in the world, it has a depth of 2,950 ft (900 m) and rims that are only 3,600 ft (1,100 m) apart. It takes 7–8 hours to walk the 6 mi (10 km) through it from Papingo to Monodendri.

5. Lying 14,436 ft (4,400 m) below its flanking peaks Dhaulagiri and Annapurna in Nepal, it is said to be the deepest valley in the world.

6. The largest land canyon on earth, it has a length of 277 mi (466 km). Hiking trails reach from both rims to Phantom Ranch in the canyon bottom.

7. One of Africa's great natural wonders, it is a canyon in Namibia over 100 mi (160 km) long and over 2,000 ft (600 m) deep in places, through which runs a 4–5-day backpacking trail.

8. Almost 10,000 ft (3,000 m) deep in places, this canyon provides the most exciting river-running in Peru. The 2-day walk through it from Cabanaconde to Chivay is becoming an increasingly popular hike.

9. Mark Twain called this 10-mi (16-km) long, almost 4,000-ft (1,200-m) deep canyon "The Grand Canyon of the Pacific." It provides some of the best hiking in Hawaii.

10. An offshoot of the Paria River Gorge in Utah, it is said to provide the best narrows or slot canyon hike in the world.

Answers

1. Hells Canyon ◆ 2. Copper Canyon ◆ 3. The Samaria Gorge ◆ 4. The Vikos Gorge ◆ 5. The Kali Gandaki ◆ 6. The Grand Canyon (of the Colorado River), Arizona ◆ 7. The Fish River Canyon ◆ 8. The Colca Canyon ◆ 9. The Waimea Canyon, Kauai ◆ 10. Buckskin Gulch

57

Potpourri 9

1. When was the first all-female ascent of Canada's Mount Logan?

    1961?   1993?   Never?

2. Where in Spanish territory can you obtain hot chocolate laced with cognac at 11,664 ft (3,555 m) on a volcano?

3. Why is it difficult to walk in a Karman Vortex Street?

4. Name the grandson of King Victor Emmanuel II of Italy, whose expeditions made the first ascents of Mount St. Elias (1897) and the Ruwenzori (1906), and reached a height of 21,800 ft (6,640 m) on K2 (1909).

5. The Slickrock Trail at Moab, Utah, US, is perhaps the world's most famous mountain-biking trail, but for what kind of vehicle was it originally designed in 1969?

6. Who were the male and female winners of both the 1992 and 1993 indoor climbing World Cup competitions?

7. How long will it take a plastic bag dropped in the wilderness to decompose?

      1–5 years?
      5–10 years?
      10–20 years?

8. While climbing the south face of Annapurna in 1970, Don Whillans found himself alone in a high camp without food until Scot Dougal Haston reached him. What was the only food that Haston had brought with him?

9. What is the Raid Gauloises?

10. How much excrement is airlifted out of the solar latrine at Trail Camp on Mount Whitney, California, every year?

      1 ton?   3 tons?   6 tons?

climbing among other activities   •   10. Six tons
a different country each year, that involves hiking and rock
annual endurance race, originated in France but taking place in
Erbesfield (US)   •   8. Porridge oats   •   9. An
•   5. The motorcycle   •   6. François Legrand (France) and Robyn
around it.   •   4. Luigi Amadeo Giuseppe, Duke of the Abruzzi
formed in the lee of a mountain when the wind divides to pass
alternating clockwise and anti-clockwise eddies of strong wind
of Tenerife   •   3. A Karman Vortex Street is a series of
1. 1993   •   2. The top cable-car station on El Teide on the island

Mountain Passes of the World

☞ **Name the following important mountain passes of the world.**

1. This is a 13,180-ft (4,020-m) pass that is the highest on California's John Muir Trail.

2. A 7,048-ft (2,148-m) pass on New Zealand's Main Divide, it is the highpoint of a challenging 3–4-day trek in Mount Cook National Park.

3. A 4,225-ft (1,288-m) pass in the Selkirks of British Columbia, it played an important part in the history of Canadian mountaineering during the years 1885 to 1916, when the Canadian Pacific Railroad crossed it and gave easy access to the mountains.

4. A 8,321-ft (2,537-m) pass on the French/Swiss border, it is the highest crossed on the 100-mi (160-km) circuit around Mont Blanc known as the Tour du Mont Blanc.

5. It is a 17,771-ft (5,417-m) pass that is the highest point reached on the trek around Annapurna.

6. A curious gap at 9,200 ft (2,804 m) in the thin wall of rock that forms the French/Spanish frontier above Gavarnie in the Pyrenees, about 300 ft (100 m) deep and 120 ft (40 m) wide, it is named after Charlemagne's nephew, who supposedly struck the rock with his magic sword when mortally wounded in battle.

7. A 15,585-ft (4,750-m) pass crossed on the Llanganuco to Santa Cruz circuit, it is Peru's second most popular long-distance trek.

8. It is an 8,548-ft (2,605-m) pass that is the highest point reached on the popular trail that links Paradise Valley to Larch Valley in the Lake Louise area of the Canadian Rockies.

9. Napoleon used this 8,100-ft (2,468-m) alpine pass to cross from Switzerland to Italy in 1800.

10. A 19,770-ft (6,026-m) pass on the Nepal/Tibet border west of Mount Everest, it was reached by Mallory from the Tibet side in 1921 when he became the first foreigner to see the Nepalese side of the mountain and look into the Western Cwm.

Answers

1. Forester Pass ✦ 2. Copland Pass ✦ 3. Rogers Pass ✦ 4. Grand Col Ferret ✦ 5. Thorong La ✦ 6. Brèche de Roland ✦ 7. Punta Union ✦ 8. Sentinel Pass ✦ 9. Great St. Bernard Pass ✦ 10. Lho La

59

Like and Unlike 3

☞ **What do the following four things have in common?**

1. Annapurna   Kamet
   Mount Everest   Nanda Devi
   Clue: first ascents

2. Chris Bonington   Wang Fu-chou
   Hisashi Ishiguro   Sharon Wood
   Clue: Himalayan climbing

3. 15,771 ft (4,807 m)   15,204 ft (4,634 m)
   14,912 ft (4,545 m)   14,853 ft (4,527 m)
   Clue: Alps

4. Fluted Peak   Island Peak
   Mera Peak   Tent Peak

5. Himavanta   Rotpunkt
   Taternik   The Iwa To Yuki

☞ **Which of the following four things is different from the other three and why?**

6. Chomolungma   Everest
   Nuptse   Sagarmatha

7. 7a (France)   7a (England)
   5.14a (US)   31 (Australia)

8. La Roche Noir   Mauna Kea
   Mont Blanc   Weisshorn
   Clue: toponymy

9. Queen Alexandra Range

   Queen Elizabeth Range

   Queen Anne
   Mountains

   Queen Maud
   Mountains

   Clue: Antarctica

10. Agincourt (France)
    Hubble (England)
    Clue: rock climbs

    Ancient Arts (US)
    Maginot Line (France)

Answers

1. Each was the highest mountain climbed in the world at the time of its first ascent. ◆ 2. They have all climbed Mount Everest. ◆ 3. The mountains with these heights (Mont Blanc, Monte Rosa, Dom, and Lyskamm) are the four highest mountains in the Alps. ◆ 4. They are all trekking peaks in Nepal. ◆ 5. They are all mountaineering journals, published in India, Germany, Poland, and Japan, respectively. ◆ 6. They are all names for Mount Everest except Nuptse, which is a neighboring mountain. ◆ 7. They are all equivalent grades of rock climb except 7a (France), which is easier than the other three. ◆ 8. They are all "white" except La Roche Noir (*Noir* = black in French, *Kea* = white in Hawaiian, *Blanc* = white in French, *Weiss* = white in German). ◆ 9. The only one that is not a mountain range in Antarctica is the Queen Anne Mountains. ◆ 10. Ancient Arts is the only one of the four rock climbs that at the time of its first ascent was not the hardest rock climb in the world. The others were all climbed by Ben Moon (England).

60

The Andes

1. Name the Andean mountain whose summit is the farthest from the center of the earth, making it by some calculations the highest mountain on earth.

2. What and where is The Fortress?

3. At approximately what height is the snow line in the Venezuelan Andes?

      8,200 ft (2,500 m)?
      11,500 ft (3,500 m)?
      14,800 ft (4,500 m)?

4. How many countries do the Andes pass through?

5. Some of the most spectacular mountain scenery in South America lies on the Chilean/Argentinean border between Puerto Montt and Bariloche, about 600 mi (1,000 km) south of Santiago. What is the popular name for this region?

6. How does an *arriero* help Andean trekkers?

7. Of what did Harold (Bill) Tilman's party make the first successful crossing in 1956?

8. Name the 8,100-ft (2,469-m) mountain in the Darwin Range of Tierra del Fuego that was formerly called Darwin I, but was renamed for a British mountaineer and explorer whose expedition climbed it in 1962.

9. Cesare Maestri returned delirious from his claimed first ascent of Cerro Torre in Patagonia in 1959, during which his partner was killed, and his claim was ques-

tioned. What was controversial about his second ascent in 1970?

10. Why would you probably run away if you encountered a *hualapichi* in the Cordillera Real of Bolivia?

Answers

1. Chimborazo, Ecuador ◆ 2. A 9,040-ft (2,755-m) peak in Patagonia, Chile ◆ 3. 11,500 ft (3,500 m) ◆ 4. Seven ◆ 5. The Lake District ◆ 6. An *arriero* is a muleteer whose mules carry trek supplies. ◆ 7. The Helio Sur or South Patagonian Ice Cap ◆ 8. Mount Shipton ◆ 9. He used a compressed air drill to drill holes in the rock for bolts. ◆ 10. A *hualapichi* is a legendary snow ghost that inhabits the Cordillera Real.

61

Films 2

1. On the face of which mountain is Cary Grant pursued by Martin Landau in Alfred Hitchcock's 1959 comedy-thriller *North by Northwest*?

2. Near which volcanic monolith does the alien spaceship land in Steven Spielberg's *Close Encounters of the Third Kind*?

3. Into which mountain range does Mad Dog Earle, played by Humphrey Bogart, escape in the 1941 film of the same name?

4. *Alive* tells the true story of a 1972 plane crash in the mountains and the epic walk out to civilization that

saved the survivors. In which mountain range did the plane crash?

5. In which Californian mountains were the location scenes for the television series *M.A.S.H.* filmed?

6. Name the mountain range that is the title of a 1990 film and the backdrop to its story, in which the Victorian explorer Sir Richard Burton searches for the source of the Nile.

7. In which disaster film about a train of plague victims approaching a weakened bridge does Martin Sheen play a mountaineer?

8. Which famous 761-ft (232-m) Hawaiian landmark is the title of a 1962 film starring Charlton Heston?

9. Which 3,041-ft (927-m) Mediterranean volcano is the title of a 1949 film starring Ingrid Bergman?

10. Name the mountain range in which Humphrey Bogart and his partners search for gold in an Oscar-winning 1948 film.

Answers

1. Mount Rushmore, South Dakota ♦ 2. The Devil's Tower, Wyoming ♦ 3. High Sierra, California ♦ 4. The Andes ♦ 5. The Santa Monica Mountains ♦ 6. *The Mountains of the Moon* ♦ 7. *The Cassandra Crossing* ♦ 8. Diamond Head ♦ 9. Stromboli ♦ 10. The Sierra Madre. The film is *Treasure of the Sierra Madre*.

62

Mountain Fauna and Flora

1. Which animal causes more injuries than any other to the world's hikers?

2. Why should the north- and south-facing slopes of a mountain support different flora?

3. What creatures, previously thought legendary, were discovered on the Muir Glacier in Alaska in 1887?

4. What is the highest elevation at which flowering plants have been seen on a mountain?

      17,000 ft (5,181 m)?

      21,000 ft (6,400 m)?

      25,000 ft (7,620 m)?

5. Fewer than 650 mountain gorillas survive in the mountains at the junction of three African countries. Name two of them (the countries, not the gorillas!).

6. Why do many high mountain plants have waxy leaves?

7. What is the canine height record on a mountain?

8. What is the highest confirmed altitude ever reached by a bird in flight?

      17,000 ft (5,181 m)?

      27,000 ft (8,229 m)?

      37,000 ft (11,277 m)?

9. Which flower appears on the badge of the Austrian Alpine Club?

10. Since records started, how many hikers in North America have been killed by wolves?

   0?   2?   11?

Answers

1. The dog • 2. Because the south-facing slopes receive more sunshine in the northern hemisphere, and vice versa in the southern hemisphere • 3. Ice worms • 4. 21,000 ft (6,400 m). *Ermania himalayensis* and *Ranunculus lobatus* were seen at this height on Kamet in 1955. • 5. Rwanda, Uganda, Zaire • 6. To reduce water loss by evaporation • 7. Several dogs have reached the 22,834-ft (6,959-m) summit of Aconcagua in Argentina. • 8. 37,000 ft (11,277 m). A Ruppell's vulture collided with an aircraft at this height in 1973; the bird was identified by its feather remains. • 9. An edelweiss • 10. Zero

Potpourri 10

1. Where is the Top of the World Provincial Park?

2. In 1911 Henry Alexander, Jr., drove a 20-horsepower car to the summit of Scotland's Ben Nevis as a publicity stunt organized by the car's American manufacturer. It took 4 days for the drive up and 2½ hours for the drive down. What was the make and model of the car?

3. Buttes and mesas are both hills that have steeply sloping, often rocky sides and flat tops. What is the difference between them?

4. What large man-made artifact was found at an altitude of about 2,100 m (7,000 ft) on Al Judi in Turkey in 1994?

5. After four unsuccessful attempts, American feminist Annie Peck Smith finally made the first ascent of the 21,833-ft (6,655-m) north peak of Huascaran in the Andes in 1908. How old was she?

   22?   47?   58?

6. What is GPS, and how does it help you determine your exact location on a mountain in bad weather?

7. The term "hard man" is sometimes applied to someone who climbs to a high standard. What did the term originally mean among nineteenth-century alpinists?

8. When you hike into the Grand Canyon, how many years into the geological past are you stepping for every foot you descend?

   1,000 years?
   200,000 years?
   1 million years?

9. What is unusual for Morocco about the 10,735-ft (3,279-m) summit of Oukaimeden?

10. How are heights measured on the moon and other planets that have no sea level?

Answers

1. In the Canadian Rockies ◆ 2. A Ford Model T ◆ 3. A butte is smaller than a mesa. A butte is often an eroded mesa, and a mesa is often an eroded plateau. ◆ 4. A boat, said by some to be Noah's Ark ◆ 5. 58 ◆ 6. The Global Positioning System (GPS) is a network of 24 satellites orbiting the earth. A hand-held portable receiver enables satellite signals to be used to pinpoint exact location anywhere on earth. ◆ 7. Someone who had lots of stamina and "went well" on the mountain ◆ 8. 200,000 years ◆ 9. It can be reached by chairlift. ◆ 10. The planet is regarded as a perfect sphere with a fixed diameter, and heights are measured relative to that. When measuring lunar heights the moon is regarded as a perfect sphere with a diameter of 1,080 mi (1,738 km).

Mountains of the World 3

👉 **Name the famous mountains of the world on which the following features are found.**

1. South Col
   Khumbu Icefall

2. Red Tower
   Moseley Slab

3. Cassin Ridge
   Muldrow Glacier

4. Grand Traverse
   Caroline Face

5. Death Bivouac
   Flatiron

Western Cwm

Hillary Step

Solvay Hut

Hörnli Ridge

Isis Face

Sourdough Couloir

Linda Glacier

Zurbriggen's Ridge

Hinterstoisser Traverse

Traverse of the Gods

6. Marangu Gate	Barranco Hut
The Saddle	Gillman's Point
7. The Great Roof	Cyclops Eye
The Heart	The Nose
8. The Magic Line	Savoia Pass
Abruzzi Ridge	Godwin-Austen Glacier
9. Dôme du Goûter	Peuterey Ridge
Brenva Face	Vallot Hut
10. Confluencia	Plaza de Mulas
The Canaleta	Nido de Condores
	(Condor's Nest)

Answers

1. Mount Everest, Nepal ◆ 2. The Matterhorn, Italy/
Switzerland ◆ 3. Denali, Alaska ◆ 4. Mount Cook, New
Zealand ◆ 5. The Eiger, Switzerland ◆ 6. Kilimanjaro,
Tanzania ◆ 7. El Capitan, California ◆ 8. K2, Pakistan
◆ 9. Mont Blanc, France/Italy ◆ 10. Aconcagua, Argentina

What and Where? 2

☞ **What and where are the following?**

1. Nun and Kun
2. The Cirque of the Unclimbables
3. The Twelve Apostles
4. The Moose's Tooth
5. Concordia
6. Batian and Nelion

7. The Big Beehive
8. Castor and Pollux
9. The Bungle Bungles
10. The Ogre

Answers

1. 23,000-ft (7,000-m) peaks in the Punjab Himalaya • 2. Spectacular granite peaks in the Logan Mountains of Canada's Northwest Territories • 3. Sea cliffs near Cape Town, South Africa • 4. A 10,355-ft (3,156-m) rock peak in the Alaska Range • 5. A spectacular and popular trekking destination at the junction of the Baltoro and Godwin-Austen glaciers near the foot of K2 • 6. The twin summits of Mount Kenya • 7. A summit and viewpoint above Lake Louise in the Canadian Rockies • 8. Neighboring 4,000-m (13,124-ft) peaks in the Alps • 9. A mountain range in Australia • 10. A 23,900-ft (7,285-m) peak in the Karakoram

66

World Alps

☞ Match each alpine mountain range in List 1 with the country in List 2 in which it can be found.

List 1

1. Alpes Montes
2. Julian Alps
3. Kita Alps
4. Maritime Alps

5. Southern Alps
6. Staunings Alps
7. Stubai Alps
8. Swabian Alps
9. Transylvanian Alps
10. Trinity Alps

List 2

a. Austria
b. France
c. Germany
d. Greenland
e. Japan
f. New Zealand
g. Romania
h. Slovenia
i. The moon
j. US

Answers

1. Alpes Montes—The moon (i) • 2. Julian Alps—Slovenia (h) • 3. Kita Alps—Japan (e) • 4. Maritime Alps—France (b) • 5. Southern Alps—New Zealand (f) • 6. Staunings Alps—Greenland (d) • 7. Stubai Alps—Austria (a) • 8. Swabian Alps—Germany (c) • 9. Transylvanian Alps—Romania (g) • 10. Trinity Alps—US (j)

67

Literary Connections 2

☞ **Name the mountain or mountain range where the action takes place in these classic mountaineering books.**

1. Walter Bonatti, *On the Heights* (1964)
2. Art Davidson, *Minus 148°* (1969)
3. Kurt Diemberger, *Summits and Secrets* (1971)
4. Norman Dyhrenfurth, *To the Third Pole* (1955)
5. Heinrich Harrer, *The White Spider* (1959)
6. Arnold Lunn, *The Mountains of Youth* (1925)
7. David Roberts, *Mountain of My Fear* (1969)
8. Galen Rowell, *In the Throne Room of the Mountain Gods* (1977)
9. Eric Shipton, *Land of Tempest* (1963)
10. Joe Simpson, *Touching the Void* (1988)

Answers

1. The Alps ◆ 2. Denali, Alaska ◆ 3. The Himalayas
◆ 4. The Himalayas ◆ 5. The Eiger, Switzerland ◆ 6. The Alps ◆ 7. Mount Huntington, Alaska ◆ 8. K2, Karakoram ◆ 9. Patagonian Andes ◆ 10. Siule Grande, Andes

68

Volcanoes

1. Name the American volcano that blew its top in 1980, reducing its height from 9,677 ft (2,951 m) to 8,365 ft (2,551 m). A hiking route up Monitor Ridge, opened in 1987, climbs to the new summit.

2. Name the peak that, with a height of almost 11,000 ft (3,350 m), is the highest volcano in Western Europe. It remains dangerously active and hikers are advised not to go all the way to the summit.

3. Orizaba (18,700 ft/5,699 m) is Mexico's highest volcano. How many days does it normally take to climb to the summit and back from the huts at the road end on its northern side?

   1 day?   2 days?   3 days?

4. The highest mountain in Portuguese territory is a 7,713-ft (2,351-m) volcano named Pico that stands on an island of the same name. The ascent is an easy hike. In which island group is Pico?

5. The record for the longest volcanic eruption in history belongs to an American volcano. The eruption began in 1983 and is still continuing, yet hikers without respiratory difficulties can cross the summit caldera on the Halemaumau Trail. Name the volcano.

6. Name the 9,320-ft (2,840-m) peak that is Chile's most active volcano. In 1971 it destroyed the village of Canaripe, but currently it can be climbed up and down in about eight hours.

7. Name the isolated 8,262-ft (2,518-m) North Island volcano, known to the Maoris as Taranaki, that is probably the most-climbed mountain in New Zealand.

8. The highest active volcano in the whole of Europe and Asia is Kliuchevskaya (15,792 ft/4,813 m) on the Kamchatka Peninsula of eastern Siberia. When were the first three ascents of Kliuchevskaya made?

    1788, 1789, and 1791?

    1788, 1935, and 1991?

    1788, 1993, and 1994?

9. Where is the "Avenue of the Volcanoes," a valley flanked by ice-capped volcanoes reaching nearly 20,000 ft (6,000 m) in height?

10. The world's largest dormant volcano is a 10,023-ft (3,057-m) peak whose name means "House of the Sun." Hikers exploring its crater on the Sliding Sands Trail have the demigod Maui to thank for the long, hot days, for it was Maui who climbed to the summit and lassoed the sun's genitals, thereby encouraging him to slow down. Name the volcano.

Answers

1. Mount St. Helens, Washington • 2. Mount Etna, Sicily, Italy • 3. 1 day • 4. The Azores • 5. Kilauea, Hawaii • 6. Volcan Villarrica • 7. Mount Egmont • 8. 1788, 1935, and 1991 • 9. Ecuador • 10. Haleakala, Hawaii

Potpourri 11

1. The Alps are "fold mountains," formed by the folding of the earth's crust. Where in the world are new fold mountains being formed at present?

2. Besides "folding," there are three other ways in which mountains are built. Name two of them.

3. Who is Samivel?

4. Studies done on long-distance backpackers on the Appalachian Trail in the eastern US show that they always lose weight, no matter how much food they carry. Why?

5. On which mountain is the highest climbers' hut in the world?

6. What was unusual about the way the 3,600-ft (1,100-m) west face of Mount Thor on Baffin Island was descended by an American/Canadian team in 1982?

7. What would you do with *Bergstiegeressen*?

8. The world's first recorded rock climb was of Mont Aiguille in France. When did this take place?

    1492?   1666?   1812?

9. Where and in what decade did modern mountain biking begin?

10. Who holds the lunar height record, having reached a height of 25,688 ft (7,830 m) on the Descartes Highlands in 1972?

Answers

Duke

1. Nowhere ◆ 2. Faulting, volcanic eruption (producing cone-shaped mountains), underground volcanic intrusion (producing dome-shaped mountains) ◆ 3. Samivel is the pen-name of a French artist and former mountaineer who is famous throughout Europe for his mountaineering drawings and cartoons. ◆ 4. The more food carried, the heavier the pack, and the more energy expended in carrying it. ◆ 5. The Refugio Independencia is at 21,477 ft (6,546 m) on Aconcagua, Argentina. ◆ 6. They dropped a long, single rope from the top to the bottom and abseiled down it. ◆ 7. Eat it. It's an inexpensive dish that guardians of German and Austrian alpine huts are required to provide on the menu for climbers who haven't much money. ◆ 8. 1492. ◆ 9. Marin County, California, in the 1970s ◆ 10. US astronauts John Watts Young and Charles Duke

70

Mountain Weather

1. *Katabatic* winds are common in mountainous areas. What are they?

2. The Beaufort scale of wind force runs from zero (calm) to eleven (64–75 mph/103–120 km/hr—violent storm), with hurricanes rated 12–17. What wind force is sufficient to impede progress when hiking?

3. Excluding tornadoes, the highest surface wind speed ever recorded was 231 mph (371 km/hr) on an American mountain. Name the mountain.

4. What is a rain shadow and what causes it?

5. Why does a cloud cap on a mountain appear stationary even in a strong wind?

6. When can you see your own glory?

7. On average, by approximately how much does temperature decrease per 1,000 ft (300 m) of altitude?

8. Wind makes temperatures seem colder than they are—a phenomenon known as wind-chill. What is the effective temperature given an air temperature of 40° F (4° C) and a wind of 40 mph (64 km/hr)?

   -10° F (-23° C)?

   10° F (-12° C)?

   25° F (-4° C)?

9. In the same weather conditions, what geographical factor besides altitude affects the temperature on a mountain?

10. Which American mountain holds the record for the most amount of snow fallen during a year, when 1,224½ in (31,102 mm) fell between February 19, 1971, and February 18, 1972?

Answers

1. Cold, gravity-induced winds that flow off mountains into valleys, especially on cold nights. ◆ 2. Eight (39-46 mph/62-74 km/hr—gale) ◆ 3. Mount Washington, New Hampshire ◆ 4. Rain on windward slopes of mountains is caused by the condensation of water vapor in rising, cooling air. A rain shadow is a region of less rain on leeward slopes where descending, warming air causes clouds to break up. ◆ 5. Because cloud continually forms at the windward edge and breaks up at the leeward edge ◆ 6. A glory is a haloed shadow of a person's head cast deep into mist by the sun. It is most often seen when walking along a mountain ridge above cloud. ◆ 7. 3.6° F (2° C) ◆ 8. 10° F (-12° C) ◆ 9. Latitude ◆ 10. Mount Rainier, Washington

71

Mountain Ranges of the World 2

👉 **Name the following mountain ranges of the world.**

1. At 4,700 mi (7,600 km) long, it is the longest mountain range on earth.

2. A range of jagged peaks on the Polish-Slovak border that is the highest mountain group in the Carpathians, its highest peak is Gerlach (8,737 ft/2,663 m).

3. Literally the "Snow Hills," this African mountain range is better known as the "Mountains of the Moon." Their present name was given to them by the explorer and journalist H. M. Stanley, after whom the highest group of tops (Mount Stanley) is named.

4. A cluster of sheer granite spires in Canada's Purcell Range, it gives some of the best rock climbing in North America. At the time of its first ascent in 1940, 10,050-ft (3,063-m) Snowpatch Spire was considered to be the continent's number-one climbing problem.

5. A small but spectacular range of limestone peaks in northern Spain, equally popular with climbers and cavers, its highest peak is Torre de Cerredo (8,668 ft /2,642 m).

6. Literally the "Dragon Mountains," but known to Zulus as the "Barrier of Spears," this rugged mountain range near the southern tip of Africa boasts 10,000-ft (3,000-m) peaks on the fringes of the Indian Ocean.

7. A mountain range that stretches for nearly 600 mi (1,000 km) between the Black Sea and the Caspian Sea, its highest peak is Elbrus (18,481 ft/5,663 m).

8. The major mountain system of Mexico, extending 1,500 mi (2,500 km) southward from the US border, its three parts enclose the Mexican plain on the west, east, and south and are consequently named Occidental, Oriental, and del Sur.

9. Literally the "Celestial Mountains," this mountain range extends for 1,000 mi (1,600 km) along the Russo-Chinese border and contains numerous 21,000-ft (6,500-m) peaks and 40-mi (70-km) long glaciers. Its highest peak is Pobeda (24,407 ft/7,439 m).

10. It is a 600-mi (1,000-km) long European mountain range that blocked the allied advance against Nazi Germany in 1944 until the Tenth Mountain Infantry Division, their piton hammers muffled with cloth, secretly scaled the heights at night and overran enemy positions. The highest peak, Corno Grande (9,583 ft/2,921 m), is an easy summer walk.

Answers

1. Andes ◆ 2. Tatra ◆ 3. Ruwenzori ◆ 4. Bugaboos ◆ 5. Picos de Europa ◆ 6. Drakensberg ◆ 7. Caucasus ◆ 8. Sierra Madre ◆ 9. Tien Shan ◆ 10. Appenines

72

Island Mountains 2

☞ **Match each mountain in List 1 with the island in List 2 of which it is the highest mountain.**

List 1

1. Agung (10,308 ft/3,142 m)
2. Blue Peak (7,388 ft/2,252 m)
3. Gros Morne (2,650 ft/806 m)
4. Hvannadalshnukur (6,952 ft/2,119 m)
5. Mayor (4,739 ft/1,445 m)
6. Olympus (6,404 ft/1,952 m)
7. Ossa (5,305 ft/1,617 m)
8. Pidurutalagala (8,280 ft/2,524 m)
9. Psiloritis (8,058 ft/2,456 m)
10. Turquino (6,500 ft/2,005 m)

List 2

a. Bali
b. Crete
c. Cuba
d. Cyprus
e. Iceland
f. Jamaica
g. Majorca
h. Newfoundland
i. Sri Lanka
j. Tasmania

73

The Himalayas 2

1. The first 8,000-m (26,247-ft) peak to be climbed was Annapurna in 1950. How many expeditions before 1950 had attempted and failed to climb an 8,000-m peak?

    8?   22?   41?

2. The first 8,000-m peak to be climbed alpine style (i.e., without porters or oxygen) was climbed by an Austrian expedition in 1957. Name the peak.

3. What was the last 8,000-m peak to be climbed, by a Chinese expedition in 1964?

4. By how much are the Himalayas rising each year?

    0.4 in (1 cm)?
    4 in (10 cm)?
    24 in (60 cm)?

5. The government of Pakistan's Ministry of Tourism lists 209 6,000-m (19,685-ft) peaks open to foreign

climbers. How many of these are unnamed?

      3?   29?   87?

6. Why did Charles Evans, leader of the first successful ascent of Kangchenjunga in 1955, call his expedition book *Kangchenjunga—The Untrodden Peak*?

7. What was the 1993 peak fee for a previously climbed 7,000-m (22,966-ft) mountain in Bhutan?

      US$1,000?   US$5,000?   US$20,000?

8. In 1978 the government of Nepal opened up to foreign climbers a number of "trekking peaks" that do not require the normal expensive expedition permits. The highest trekking peak has a height of 21,248 ft (6,476 m) and is technically easy. Name it.

9. The trek around Annapurna is one of the most popular in the Himalayas. What is the normal trek time?

      2 weeks?   3½ weeks?   5 weeks?

10. What is the Himalayan Club?

Answers

1. 22 • 2. Broad Peak • 3. Shisha Pangma • 4. 0.4 in (1 cm) • 5. 87 • 6. Kangchenjunga is a sacred Tibetan mountain, and the summit climbers turned back 5 ft from the summit in order not to offend their Sherpas. • 7. US$20,000 • 8. Mera Peak • 9. Three and a half weeks • 10. An Indian-based club, formed in 1928 from the original Himalayan Club and the Mountain Club of India, whose aim is to encourage Himalayan climbing and exploration

Good Seconds

The mountains in List 1 all fail by one to be the highest in their country. Match each with the country in List 2 of which it is the second highest.

List 1

1. Ben Macdui (4,294 ft/1,309 m)
2. Dom (14,911 ft/4,544 m)
3. Glittertind (8,045 ft/2,452 m)
4. Illimani (21,201 ft/6,462 m)
5. Mount Foraker (17,402 ft/5,304 m)
6. Mount Lucania (17,147 ft/5,226 m)
7. Mount Smolikas (8,652 ft/2,637 m)
8. Mount Tasman (11,475 ft/3,498 m)
9. Mount Townsend (7,252 ft/2,210 m)
10. Yerupaja (21,759 ft/6,632 m)

List 2

a. Australia
b. Bolivia
c. Canada
d. Greece
e. New Zealand
f. Norway
g. Peru
h. Switzerland
i. United Kingdom
j. United States

Answers

1. Ben Macdui—United Kingdom (i)   •   2. Dom—Switzerland (h)
•   3. Glittertind—Norway (f)   •   4. Illimani—Bolivia (b)
•   5. Mount Foraker—United States (j)   •   6. Mount Lucania—
Canada (c)   •   7. Mount Smoilkas—Greece (d)   •   8. Mount
Tasman—New Zealand (e)   •   9. Mount Townsend—Australia (a)
•   10. Yerupaja—Peru (g)

75

Potpourri 12

1. During the winter of 1924–25, how did Albert MacCarthy and his team get ten tons of supplies 140 mi (225 km) to the base of Canada's Mount Logan, in preparation for their attempt on the summit?

2. What is the origin of the term "tiger," as formerly used to describe a good mountaineer?

3. Which famous fifteenth-century Italian painter reached a height of 10,000 ft (3,000 m) on Monte Rosa in the Alps and, as a result, concluded that glaciers were made from layers of hail?

4. Which provides more lasting energy?
   Fruit?   Nuts?   Chocolate?

5. Why are some river valleys V-shaped and some U-shaped?

6. Name the landscape photographer who lived from 1902 to 1984 and whose black-and-white prints did much to publicize the grandeurs of Yosemite, California.

7. How did "La Montagne" (The Mountain) take part in the 1789 French Revolution?

8. What is *andinismo*?

9. Two bridges for the use of hikers and mule trains cross the Colorado River in the depths of the Grand Canyon: the Black Bridge and the Silver Bridge. Hikers use both bridges, but mules refuse to cross the Silver Bridge. Why?

10. Would you recommend this book to your friends?

Answers

1. They used sleds drawn by dog teams and horses.
♦ 2. The name was originally given to the 15 Sherpas who reached the North Col and beyond on the 1924 British Everest Expedition. ♦ 3. Leonardo da Vinci! 4. Nuts ♦ 5. River valleys are normally eroded by rivers into a V-shape, unless a glacier grinds them down and carves them into a U-shape. ♦ 6. Ansel Adams ♦ 7. La Montagne was the name of the extreme democratic party, whose leaders included Danton and Robespierre. ♦ 8. The Andean equivalent of alpinism ♦ 9. Its open construction enables them to see the river beneath them. ♦ 10. Yes.